the way she feels

MY LIFE ON THE BORDERLINE
IN PICTURES AND PIECES

Courtney Cook

 TIN HOUSE / Portland, Oregon

Published by Tin House, Portland, Oregon
Distributed by W. W. Norton & Company

Library of Congress Cataloging-in-Publication Data

Names: Cook, Courtney, 1995- author.
Title: The way she feels : my life on the borderline in pictures and pieces
  / Courtney Cook.
Description: Portland, Oregon : Tin House, [2021]
Identifiers: LCCN 2020057436 | ISBN 9781951142599 (paperback) | ISBN
  9781951142605 (ebook)
Subjects: LCSH: Cook, Courtney, 1995- | Borderline personality
  disorder--United States--Biography--Comic books, strips, etc. | LCGFT:
  Autobiographical comics.
Classification: LCC RC569.5.B67 C666 2021 | DDC 616.85/852 [B]--dc23
LC record available at https://lccn.loc.gov/2020057436

First US Edition 2021
Printed in China
Interior design by Diane Chonette
Illustrations by Courtney Cook

www.tinhouse.com

To 13-year-old Courtney,
who never thought she'd make it this far.

Hey there! Thanks so much for reading. Before you begin, I just want to give you a heads-up—this book deals with some heavy topics, including (but not limited to) self-harm, mental illness, and suicide. I've taken great care to ensure the subject matter is dealt with in a compassionate and respectful manner, but understand that some readers may find it troubling. Please take care of yourself!
National Suicide Prevention Lifeline:
800-273-8255
Crisis text line:
Text "HELLO" to 741741
National Institute of Mental Health:
Nimh.Nih.gov

Contents

The Blow-Dryer Is Full of Souls and Other Facts in Lists

The basics:

- Courtney Leigh Cook

- Leigh pronounced like "Lee," not "Lay"

- Nicknamed: Bonker, CC, Coco

- MFA candidate, studying nonfiction

- Twenty-four years old

- Blond hair

- Blue eyes

- Five foot three

- Twelve tattoos, mostly on my arms

Who I am according to:

- The Myers-Briggs test: INFP

- Astrology: a Libra (Leo rising, Libra moon)

- The year I was born: a millennial

- Spotify: a listener of Midwest emo

- BuzzFeed: a contemplative introvert (as determined by my choices in salad toppings)

- Instagram ads: an admirer of Scandinavian home design

What I enjoy:

- Writing (poetry, nonfiction, lists)

- Drawing (digitally)

- Painting (gouache or watercolor)

- Reading (nonfiction)

- Binge-watching TV (Hulu > Netflix)

- Napping
  - Being constantly tired is a side effect of my medication

Why I am on medication:

- I was diagnosed with major depressive disorder and generalized anxiety disorder when I was thirteen

Definition of depression:

- According to *Merriam-Webster*: "a state of feeling sad," or "a serious medical condition in which a person feels very sad, hopeless, and unimportant and often is unable to live in a normal way"

- According to the National Institute of Mental Health: "a common but serious mood disorder. It causes severe symptoms that affect how you feel, think, and handle daily activities, such as sleeping, eating, or working."

Definition of generalized anxiety disorder:

- According to the Anxiety and Depression Association of America: "persistent and excessive worry about a number of different things"

courtney
@c00kc0

Me, a girl with anxiety: *walks downstairs, sees a grandfather clock we've had my whole life*
My brain: that clock is alive
Me: ?????
My brain: it's also evil
Me: !!!????

4/30/18, 10:04 PM

What are the symptoms of *my* depression and anxiety?

- I can turn anything into something terrifying

- Everything feels heavy and like I'm swimming through molasses

- I can cry at anything
  - By "anything" I mean "everything"

- I'm convinced most things are trying to kill me

Things that have tried to kill me:

- The blue stuff they use to stop you from bleeding when they accidentally cut you at the nail salon

- Like half of a half of a half of a bump of cocaine

- A weird string in my sock that keeps annoying my toes

- The dark because it makes the air look like flies

- The blow-dryer because it feels like souls are coming out of it

- My bathroom mirror because Bloody Mary lives in there and I've probably accidentally summoned her with my fear

- Paper cuts because I might bleed to death

- The sound of the ocean because there is an incoming tsunami and I don't have an escape plan

When I say "things that have tried to kill me," I mean:

- Things that have given me a panic attack

- Things my brain works really hard to convince me are murderous

How I cope with the things that are trying to kill me:

- Lexapro (bae forever #1 ✦ ✦ ✦)

- Beta-blockers (not as good as Lexapro but better than nothing)

- Therapy

- Singing a song to conjure a different Mary instead of Bloody Mary, such as Mary from "Mary Had a Little Lamb" (this makes sense in my head)

- Putting my back against a wall while blow-drying my hair so the souls cannot get to me (also makes a lot of sense in my head)

- Using dialectical behavior therapy (DBT) skills

- Yelling at myself

Example of yelling at myself:

- My brain: Bloody Mary lives in the mirror. Don't close your eyes; just let soap get in them. Tears are better than death, and this is life or death (even though you're definitely going to die).

- Me, to my brain: Shut up, you pussy. It's probably just the cocktail. Summon the cocktail. You don't even like Bloody Marys. You're embarrassing and more lame than your vision of Bloody Mary, which is the evil witch from Snow White. Shut up. Shut the fuck up ¯_(ツ)_/¯

How often this works:

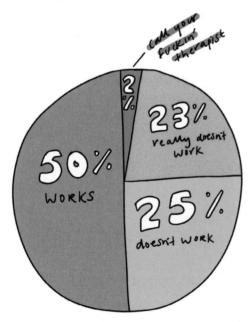

What I do when yelling doesn't work, in order of how often I utilize each strategy (from most to least often):

1. Nap
2. Call my mom
3. Cry
4. Pluck my eyebrows
5. Lie in my bed and stare at the ceiling
6. Get a new tattoo
7. Ask my friends to take me to the hospital
8. Consult a psychic
9. Spontaneously adopt a dog

Why I ask my friends to take me to the hospital:

- I am scared
- I want to be sedated
- I understand being sedated would be better than feeling this scared

How many times I've asked to be taken to the hospital:

- Five

How many times my friends have agreed to take me to the hospital:

- Zero

What they do instead:

- Listen to me cry

- Give me half a bar of Xanax and tell me to chill

- Let me nap while I make them wake me up every half hour to see if I am still alive

- Force me to journal

Example of a journal entry from one of these moments:

The world is yelling at me. It feels like I'm underwater and everything is far away and hazy. When people speak to me, it's in slow motion, comically low in pitch and drawn out, but I'm the only one who hears it that way. I'm stuck, spinning in place, sinking deeper, about to hurl from the sickness of it all and explode from the pressure. There's no air left in the universe. I want to die so this feeling stops, but the whole reason I'm feeling this way is because I'm worried I'm dying and I desperately don't want to. The world keeps moving on.

A typical day's moods:

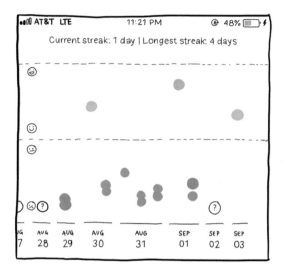

Things that have made me track my emotions as blue (depressed) or purple (sad):

- My cat looking at me in a way that felt wrong/mean?

- My high school boyfriend getting a new girlfriend like three years after we broke up, because he should love me forever even though I never think about him

- Not getting a bid from any of the thirteen sororities I rushed even though I had previously stated that I thought sororities were sexist and racist institutions

What I've done about these feelings:

- Wanted to kill myself

- Felt dramatic about them making me want to kill myself

- Cried (a lot)

- Pushed friends away before they could push me away first, or held on way too intensely so they couldn't leave

Dumb reasons why I've lost friendships:

- I didn't pay my roommate for her broken bong, which she accused me of breaking, even though I didn't break the stupid bong

- I moved out of a rat-infested co-op into an apartment, which made my BFF call me an "elitist piece of shit"

- I thought I wasn't being invited to a big sleepover when really they just hadn't invited me yet and I made such a scene I then actually wasn't invited

- I said that I didn't know that a snakeskin skirt could match differently patterned snakeskin boots

- I felt like they just *didn't get me*
  - I also don't *get* myself

Why these things are so upsetting:

- When I first meet someone, I think, *This is it*

- I picture the person being my maid of honor or my wife or my husband within like three minutes of us meeting
  - I think the person is The One™

- When the person is not The One™, I feel like I'm starting all over
  - Even if we didn't make it that far in the first place

Why I feel these things at all:

- ...

- I am afraid to tell you

Why am I afraid?

- There is a lot of stigma surrounding my Actual Problem™

Please?

- Fine.

-

-

-

-

-

- I have borderline personality disorder
  - Diagnosed at twenty-three, speculated about since thirteen
  - BPD isn't diagnosed under the age of eighteen
  - A lot of the symptoms are attributed to "growing up" before this age

Borderline personality disorder symptoms:

- Unstable relationships with other people

- Unstable emotions

- Unstable sense of self

- Feelings of emptiness

- Extreme fear of abandonment

What symptoms I have:

- The up-and-down emotions

- And the unstable sense of self

- And the feelings of emptiness

- And the extreme fear of abandonment

- Okay, fine

- Literally all of them
  - Especially the fear of abandonment though

In my own words?

- When I look back at myself, I feel like I spent most of it in a dressing room, trying different versions of myself on

- I don't understand what makes me *me*
  - Is it my interests?
  - What I dislike?
  - How people perceive me?

- My moods are tumultuous at best
  - I feel hollow inside
  - I feel like everyone probably hates me
  - At the same time, I feel like I am also maybe the best person ever

What causes borderline?

- No one really knows

- But probably a combination of childhood trauma and familial predisposition

Definition of trauma:

- According to *Oxford*: "deeply distressing or disturbing experience," or "physical injury"

- According to the American Psychiatric Association's *Diagnostic and Statistical Manual* (*DSM*): "exposure to actual or threatened death, serious injury, or sexual violence"

Relevant trauma I've experienced:

- When I was born, mismatched forceps were used to birth me. Instead of gently pulling me from the birth canal, they crushed my skull in five places, causing depressed fractures that had to be corrected with major neurosurgery.

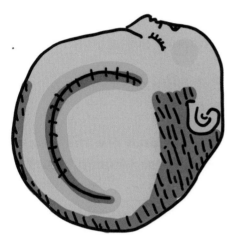

Key details:

- Doctors didn't collectively agree that babies had the capacity to feel pain until 1999. They asserted that the neural pathways necessary for pain hadn't been developed and wouldn't be until twelve months old

  - Because it was 1995, I wasn't given morphine or any pain medication that would be expected after neurosurgery

  - I was given Tylenol for two days, then no medication thereafter

- An article about the work of Michelle A. Fortier, PhD and licensed clinical psychologist, states that unmanaged pain can cause "prolonged changes to somatosensory function and hypersensitivity or decreased sensitivity to painful stimuli"

  - In layman's terms, persistent, unmanaged pain fundamentally changes the way the body perceives stimuli, painful or not

  - These changes can last long into adulthood, rewiring the sufferer's brain

What happens when one is exposed to trauma as a child?

- Citing a Harvard psychiatry professor, the article "The Long Life of Early Pain," published in the Harvard Mahoney Neuroscience Institute's letter *On the Brain*, explains: "Early-life traumatic stress and untreated pain may seriously affect a child's development, contributing to lifelong emotional disorders, including anxiety and depression, learning disabilities, and other problems in growth and development"

Do I believe my birth caused my borderline?

- Maybe

- It's hard to say

- Sort of

- On some days,
  - yes

- On some days,
  - no

Now that you know my deepest secret, do you feel like you know me? Check one.

- ☐ Yes
- ☐ No
- ☐ Sort of

Do I feel like I know myself?

- The answer is still no

- But I do know all of the above!

Is that good enough?

- It'll have to be

What's my plan for the rest of the day/week/month/year?

- Survive

This Is Why I'm Crying

I'm crying because the Mars rover *Curiosity* sings "Happy Birthday" to itself every year. I don't know what to do with my hands or whether to smile or look down when people sing me "Happy Birthday." Is crying an okay response? When I get overwhelmed, I cry, and oh yeah, I'm crying because on my dead friend's last birthday she blew out the same birthday candles that I do every year, ones that start in a closed tulip and then unfurl into tens of bursting lights that sing "Happy birthday to you" and won't stop singing until you cut a wire. I didn't know that the first time I used one and it sang in the garage trash can for three days until I looked up how to make it stop. I wish we'd never cut the wire to her candle so it could still sing for her.

I'm crying because there is a whale that speaks at a frequency no other whale can hear, but still it speaks and speaks and all the other whales hear silence. I'm crying because I'm thinking about what it would be like to be a body in the middle of the ocean. I'm thinking about a movie I watched on a plane where a girl and her boyfriend go sailing and there's a storm and she talks to him for the rest of the ninety minutes until she's saved and it's revealed that he's been dead the whole time and she was hallucinating. I'm crying because four boys from my town drowned in an icy lake on New Year's a few years ago when their canoe overturned. I pictured them smoking in the canoe at midnight. My dad said, "Imagine being the last one to go under and knowing what's next," and I cried for three days straight.

I'm crying because I painted red, cut-like lines with watercolor in my journal next to photos of cigarettes and said, "It's one or the other," and then apologized to my mom and my dead grandpa who died from smoking. That grandpa came to my mom in a dream once right before I tried to drown myself and said, "Where Courtney's going, she can't come back," and I guess that's true, only then how did he come and tell her?

I tried to drown myself in a bathtub. Tried to scrub away my hurt and my life. It didn't work, so I cried instead. Cried until the hot water turned cold. Did you know the smell of freshly cut grass is the smell of the grass trying to heal itself? I came out of the bath smelling like hotel soap, all hibiscus and fresh-ness. No one knew my soaping had been an attempt at an ending. Everyone just thought I smelled good. Everyone just thought my eyes were red from the soap.

My dog's fur was red. When he ran away, I cried for three days straight, then I got a call from a stranger who said his body was on the side of the road. I packed a cardboard box full of blankets and his favorite toys, and when I went to retrieve him, his head was flat and a wall of his smell hit me. I cried so hard I dry-heaved into the grass, feeling the flies from his body buzz around my arms. I had to call animal control to pick him up and scrape him off the road. When I called later and asked for his collar back, they told me they'd done a mass cremation and thrown away the collar. I wanted it as proof: *Here, look: this is why I'm crying.*

I'm crying because I can't stop thinking about the deer I saw get hit by a car when I was seventeen. Her legs splayed out and she ran broken into the forest and I got so scared that I called 911 and they told me, "This isn't an emergency," and I wanted to scream, "Yes, it is," but instead I cried. When I went home, I wrote a poem about her. It didn't begin this way, but if I ever rewrite it, it will begin, "This is why I'm crying."

God Circle

My mom told me about the God Circle when I was in the third grade.

I FELT ALONE

ABANDONED by friends I'd made the year before.

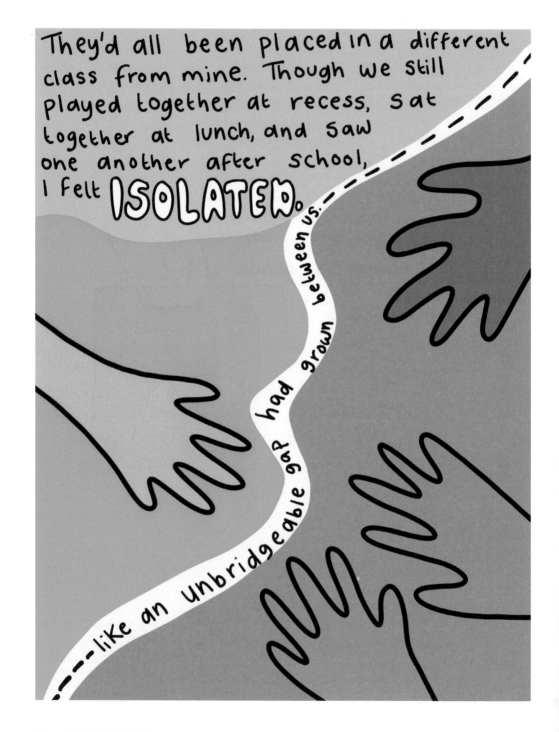

A DIAGRAM:

hang every six months friends

only when you're happy friends

so close I can taste it friends

GOD circle

your God circle is composed of friends who will last a lifetime — they're the friends you'd die for. The friends who understand you.

I LOOKED UP AND THOUGHT to Myself:

Somewhere out there, there's someone just like me.

But the thought
didn't end there.

In my desperation
I obsessed over
my mom's words

I clung to them as if
my life depended on it.

I looked for a friendship that felt **FATED**, like the Gemini twins. Someone to prove to me I was capable of the love and acceptance I craved. Someone who would mend the parts of me that were broken. Someone to **HEAL ME.**

I watched in awe as my mom's God Circle Weathered

CANCER,

DIVORCE.

yet I couldn't get, or stay, close to anyone.

What was

WRONG

with me?

everything changed when I was diagnosed with

BORDERLINE

fourteen years after learning about the God circle.

I didn't need someone to fix or heal me...

I was capable of HEALING MYSELF.

In therapy, I've worked hard to learn that the God Circle isn't

MAGIC OR **MYTHIC**

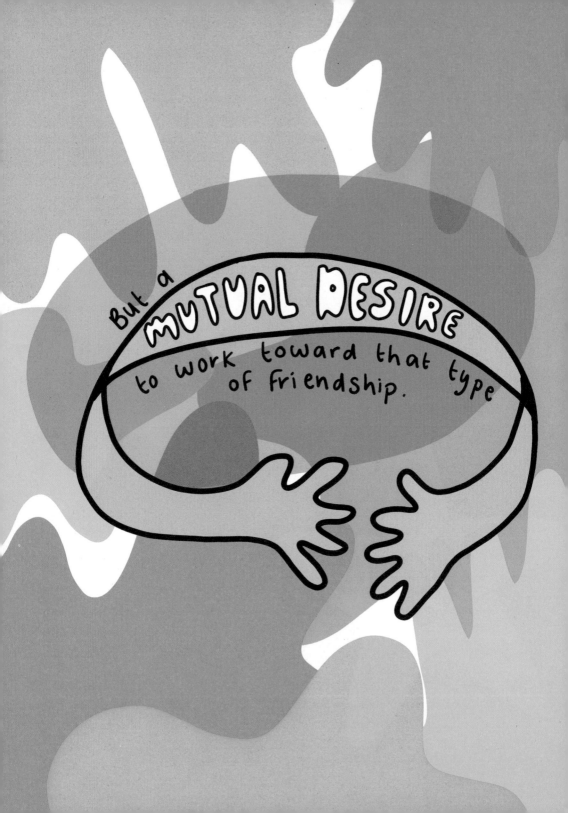

unreasonable times BPD told me I was being abandoned

1. My friends hadn't invited me to a sleepover yet before I found out about it, so despite their intentions to invite me, I accused them of abandoning me and believed everyone secretly (or openly) hated me.

2. My friends had started a group chat prior to me knowing them that they continued to use rather than only using the new one I was included in.

3. My friends ran into eachother at CVS and I somehow managed to be angry I wasn't "invited"?????

4. My boyfriend had to go to his niece's birthday party instead of coming over to get stoned and watch Gilmore Girls.

5. My friends from another school went on a senior service trip to Hawaii, and I, not a student at that school, couldn't come with.

Show Me a Happy Person and
I'll Show You a Liar

My then-boyfriend once told me as we ate pizza at a restaurant inside a converted Airstream camper.

It was summertime in Chicago and the city had finally thawed out, unearthing bicyclists and dog walkers and peonies from the snow and salt. I'd hoped my seasonal depression would also melt away and leave a rejuvenated version of myself. Instead, I was just as sad as I'd been when it got darker earlier. I had to remind myself that while the word "seasonal" precedes the name of my diagnosis during the winter months, I am left with regular depression when the season changes. At least in the winter I have something to blame for the pit in my stomach, the endless feeling of dread. In the summer, I have no reason.

The restaurant bustled around us, and I traced the word "Don't" onto the skin of my thigh with my fingernail. "Don't." Present tense. I wanted to laugh at his naiveté–that there was a place in this world where sadness doesn't exist–but instead, I imagined the town: safe enough that you weren't required to lock your doors at night, wealthy enough that you never had to go to bed hungry and always had a gift waiting for you on holidays, big enough to surprise you but small enough to feel familiar. Good schools. Big backyards. A yearly parade on the Fourth of July. Always snow on Christmas.

It was the town I grew up in.

Yet there I was, in all my depressed glory, eating pizza and intermittently wanting to kill myself. I was reminded of a straitlaced woman who approached my mom at a party years ago, thanking her–genuinely–for my at-the-time very recent and very public mental breakdown. "We all have our shit," she'd said. "Some of us are just better at hiding it."

I grew up in a small village sixteen miles north of Chicago called Winnetka. Winnetka is the type of town you might expect to see in movies–and you have. *Home Alone*, *Ferris Bueller's Day Off*, *Sixteen Candles*–they were all filmed where I grew up. Winnetka is just as idyllic as the films made it seem. The roads are paved perfectly, the town is impeccably landscaped, country clubs are within a few miles' distance in any direction, and there are ordinances requiring buildings to look uniform. When McDonald's moved to town, it wasn't allowed its golden arches. Santa comes to the local ice-skating rink every Christmas, and the Fourth of July fireworks show brings crowds from towns over. The biggest scandal to come out of Winnetka during my childhood

was when the right arm of crucified Jesus kept falling from the local church into the bushes below.

When I was growing up, my mom worked from home and played with me all day long. My dad worked in downtown Chicago and rose early so that when I returned from school he was home from work and ready to coach softball practice or help me with my math homework. We had dinner as a family, and often gathered in the living room after to watch *The Amazing Race* or *Survivor* before going to Dairy Queen to get soft serve. Before bed, my mom would read to my sister and me until we fell asleep, my sister always before me.

My house was white with a red front door and I had my own room with a small playroom attached, my own little hideaway. I played on the swing set in my backyard until my sister and I outgrew it and it was replaced by a trampoline. My two best friends lived on my block, and we'd ride our bikes or try to skateboard until it got dark, when we retired inside and watched movies until it was time to go home. We had block parties where all the neighbor kids gathered for hula-hoop contests and water balloon fights while the adults drank beer and grilled hot dogs. My family's golden retriever, Murphy, often got loose but was known around the neighborhood and, after playing with another dog for a while, he would come trotting or be delivered home.

Still, it's hard for me to remember a time when I felt truly, unmistakably happy. My memories are clouded with anxiety, recalled through a lens of fear. Though I was a child with everything I could dream of and more, I felt a gaping hole inside me that nothing tangible could fill.

A key symptom in borderline personality disorder is a chronic feeling of emptiness. The other day I walked to the fridge for the fifth time in an hour and thought to myself, *What void am I trying to fill?* It was a dumb question. I know the void. The void is the pit in my stomach that I can never fill, no matter how many bowls of cereal and pints of Ben & Jerry's Americone Dream I eat. The feelings of abandonment when someone, after spending three days straight with me, has to go home. The frustration I feel when a partner is on top of me but I need the person closer, want our bodies to merge into one. When I get a text back but need a thousand. When I get attention but need a world of it. When I'm loved but it still isn't enough.

What do you do when you're given everything and still feel empty? The problem is, my wants are intangible, a cosmic longing for something unattainable. I am always reaching for more, but "more" is generally for someone who doesn't love me to love me back, or for the entire world to think I'm special, or for everyone who meets me to fall in love with me. In other words, my "more" can't exist. My "more" is impossible. My "more" eats away at me from the inside.

I have been given all I could ever ask for, but not the one thing I want, which is everything. "Everything" in the sense that I need to be cared for in a way that is impossible. I remind myself I am lucky to live this life, and rationally, I know I am. I know that I am unfathomably lucky to have been brought up in the town I was brought up in, in the family I am a part of, to live the life I lead now. I am paid to write. I have an unending support system, people who listen with minimal judgment to every illogical and irrational thought I have, who validate me and call me on my shit. I have a dog who only sometimes pees on the carpet. I have a house filled with books I'll never have the time to read.

The one thing I don't have, however, is my mind. My mind is both mine and a stranger's, something I understand intimately and don't understand at all. I am lucky (there's that word again) to have undergone over ten years of mental health treatment that has helped me to be able to recognize when I am having borderline thoughts, or when my depression is telling me lies, like that I'm unlovable or a burden. I can recognize these moments and call myself out on them, use my rational brain to talk myself down, but I still have a ledge to be talked down from. I am constantly pulling myself off it, begging myself not to jump. *No, they don't hate you because they couldn't hang out. No, you do not annoy everyone you come into contact with. No, you are not worthless.*

I want to live a life where, for just one day, I feel full. I want to be happy and not question whether it is real. I want to feel love and not worry that everyone else feels more acutely than I do. I want to have the lights flicker without wondering if I'm being haunted. I want to cough without worrying that I am dying. I want to look in the mirror without thinking that I am fat. I want to be told "I love you" and not question it, even for a second. I want to hang out with friends and not fear that I'm missing something better somewhere else. I want to not even think of the possibility of "better." I want things to feel good the way they are.

Seneca said, "For if we could be satisfied with anything, we should have been satisfied long ago." I was born into a world of luck, a world where I was given everything, but that doesn't stop the hunger, always, for more.

Not Borderline as in "Crazy," Borderline as in "Fuck You"

There are certain things in the world that go unnoticed until your attention is called to them, like when you learn a particular word and suddenly begin to hear it everywhere. It's always existed–been said around you hundreds of times–but now feels shiny, new, neon.

When I was diagnosed with borderline personality disorder, it became a ghost that followed me around. Borderline popped up in my conversations, shocked me by existing in texts I was reading, scared me by appearing on TV.

I felt haunted, and borderline's spirit wasn't benevolent. To be borderline meant one was unstable, obsessive, dysfunctional, overly attached, simultaneously avoidant, and prone to outbursts fueled by anger. My borderline ghost, it seemed, should have been named Crazy–and in ways, it was. The representations of borderline characters in the media were from shows with the word "crazy" or its synonyms in the title; programs such as *Maniac*, movies called *Fatal Attraction*, *Mad Love*, and *Shame*. Every story was one I didn't, couldn't, aspire to; a narrative that portrayed borderline as an unconquerable, maddening disease where the sufferer was undeniably a "maniac."

Looking up famous individuals didn't help either, my results returning with names such as Amy Winehouse, the singer and songwriter who struggled immensely during her life and died tragically by her own hand, and Jeffrey Dahmer, notorious serial killer who raped, dismembered, and ate his victims. There was no one, nothing, to look toward, no example of someone living a functional life or not suffering and dying at age twenty-seven or being a fucking murderer.

I remembered being young–maybe nine or ten–and overhearing my dad and his best friend laughing at the best friend's ex-wife's seemingly desperate, erratic behavior. They called her "borderline." It was the first time I'd ever heard the word, and though I didn't know what it meant, they said it with a bite that could be heard through their laughter.

Not long after I was diagnosed, I moved to Riverside, California, to pursue an MFA in creative writing. Lonely in a new city, I took any opportunity to make a new friend, though few chances arose because most of the people in my program were considerably older than I was. When a foreign exchange student at my school messaged me, I was thrilled that someone had reached out.

Though we didn't have much in common, I was willing to push this fact aside if it meant I could have a friend my own age. It would be nice,

I told myself, to have company when shopping or at the pool, even if the relationship was superficial.

On the car ride home from the market we discovered a mutual love for true crime, and she told me that her former coworker had recently been apprehended for multiple rapes and murders. "He's borderline though, so it makes sense," she said. I sank into myself, still forty-five minutes left in our drive, and quietly said, "Wow, that's wild," before turning up the music.

I finally understood why my mom had said, "I would keep that to yourself," when I told her about my diagnosis. She'd said the name "borderline personality disorder" made the disease seem scarier than it is in actuality, and encouraged me not to tell anyone, even my closest friends. I knew it came from a place of her wanting to protect me, and in that moment in the car, her reasoning made sense. The world really does think that to have borderline is to be "crazy," and not in the casual, offhand ways people use the word when they're describing assertive women in the workplace or ex-girlfriends.

They mean crazy like Dahmer, or the Zodiac Killer.

But what does it mean to be crazy? *Merriam-Webster* defines "crazy" as "full of cracks or flaws" or "not mentally sound: insane, impractical, erratic, unusual." If this is true, then aren't I indeed crazy? Borderline personality disorder used to be known as unstable personality disorder, and is characterized by an unstable sense of self or identity disturbances, tumultuous interpersonal relationships, a persistent feeling of emptiness, and impulsive behavior. To be borderline is, by definition, to suffer from erratic moods that cause a person to be unsound and make impractical decisions, the word "disturbed" integral to diagnosis. What is being crazy if not differing from the norm in a fierce way, as borderlines inherently do?

If this is the case, is being "crazy" inherently bad? Can all the people who experience borderline personality disorder, by some estimates up to 3 percent of the population, who live mostly normal, albeit often tumultuous, lives, be bad?

Though I hate the stereotypes of borderline that are perpetuated by the media, and even exacerbated at times by my friends and family, sometimes having borderline does make me feel I deserve this label. When I am at my worst, I almost want to yell at everyone who uses "borderline" and "crazy" synonymously and tell them they're right.

When my anxiety reaches a peak so high that I interpret my SiriusXM radio cutting out as a sign the world is ending; when I am so depressed that even suicide feels like an unimaginable chore; when a friend runs into another friend at the grocery store and I convince myself they're deciding they no longer love or want to be associated with me—I know that my brain is broken. I am the human embodiment of "not mentally sound," making assumptions that would seem "insane" to anyone but me, because the thoughts that fuel them are just as unfounded. Like *Merriam-Webster* says, I am "full of cracks or flaws."

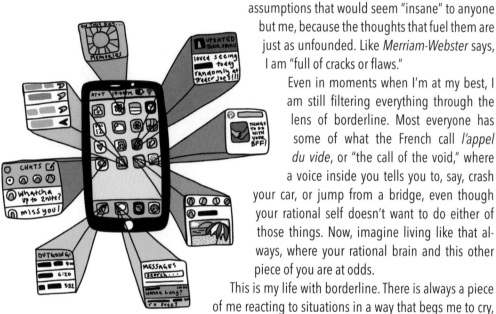

Even in moments when I'm at my best, I am still filtering everything through the lens of borderline. Most everyone has some of what the French call *l'appel du vide*, or "the call of the void," where a voice inside you tells you to, say, crash your car, or jump from a bridge, even though your rational self doesn't want to do either of those things. Now, imagine living like that always, where your rational brain and this other piece of you are at odds.

This is my life with borderline. There is always a piece of me reacting to situations in a way that begs me to cry, or make a scene, or do something impulsive, or hurt myself. Most often, it takes all my strength to make that other voice be quiet; this is my best-case scenario.

I can take my mom's advice, choose not to tell anyone about my diagnosis, but to be borderline is to be myself. People often say "You're not your illness" or "Your illness doesn't define you" when speaking about mental afflictions, but to say that I'm not borderline as much as I am Courtney is to misspeak. Borderline is a personality disorder that shapes my personality. All my actions and thoughts and emotions are filtered through my borderline brain. Even if I don't tell anyone about my diagnosis, by simply existing I am outing myself as someone with borderline personality disorder. It's more than a haunting—it's a full-on possession.

Despite my awareness of borderline's possession of my entire being, it is, oddly, still invisible to most. It is not like a missing limb, or an ostomy bag peeking from below clothing; rather, it's something I have to garner the courage to admit before it declares itself. Though my behaviors often scream "borderline," if one were unfamiliar with the disorder, one wouldn't know to associate it with me. Most likely, I'd be seen, at times, as "erratic," or "strange," or perhaps "batshit."

While many mental illnesses are more accepted in current culture than they were previously, borderline occupies a category of its own. Most people seem to understand when someone is too depressed to get out of bed, or too anxious to go to a party, but the same individuals question a person who feels abandoned when a friend is unable to hang out. A person without borderline recognizes legitimate, valid reasons why a friend or loved one might not be available, but to someone who is borderline, it's the long-awaited proof of being secretly hated, of being inevitably left behind.

Though very real parts of the disorder, these symptoms of borderline are treated as irrational, "crazy." They aren't seen as excusable, or as something that can be understood. As a result, they aren't symptoms you admit to, and they certainly aren't symptoms you expect sympathy for.

There is no greeting card for my ghost.

•

When I moved and began searching for a new therapist, eight turned me down before I found one who would work with me. Because of the symptoms that individuals with borderline have, the mental health community has deemed us manipulative, treatment-resistant, attention-seeking, and—at worst—dangerous; as a result, and those who might be able to offer treatment are often reluctant to work with us. But what is one supposed to do when even psychiatrists and therapists have deemed one "crazy"? Where else is there to turn? Sometimes I stand in front of the mirror, trying to identify my "crazy." I look at myself and try to parse out borderline from Courtney, pull it out like a splinter or infected appendix. I want to be able to point to it and say, "This is the part of me that is broken," and extract it so that I can be left with a "normal," "sane" person in its place.

But I have never known who that person may be. Though the symptoms of borderline typically rear their head when one is a teenager or entering one's twenties (diagnosis is nearly impossible under the age of eighteen), borderline behaviors have been with me for as long as I can remember. I don't know what it's like not to be borderline, and I don't have an understanding of who I'd be without it. As with a weaving that would fall apart if a single string were removed, there is no original part of myself for me to revert to, no "before" Courtney to look back on wistfully.

This is because the ghost of borderline follows me everywhere, turning my world into a haunted house where nothing is as it first appears. I make a new friend and suddenly, *Boo! They're going to abandon you*. I feel happy for a few days, maybe even weeks, and then, *Boo! Here comes the empty feeling again*. Really, the only thing I can depend on is that the house will stay haunted. No matter how long I go without symptoms, or how optimistic I might feel, there is always a ghost waiting for me, calling me back to my unwanted home.

Trying Myself On

I look back and I don't recognize myself.

there are full years where I am a stranger.

maybe that's just about what anyone knows at twenty-four.

maybe that can be enough.

The Way She Feels

Standing in the shower, I enjoyed the hot sting of the water running over my skin and turned the temperature up higher, almost scalding. The faucet maxed out at 110 degrees, and I turned it until it wouldn't turn any farther. It was December and I felt numb, from the inside out. Something inside me seemed to have broken since I'd turned thirteen, and it was like I felt nothing at all. Everything was muted, like I was making my way through molasses or listening underwater. The burning water came as a relief, a jolt of mild pain amid the nothingness. Still, my skin adjusted quickly, and I was left bathed in warmth. I picked up a hot-pink razor, placed it on my shin, took a deep breath, pressed down hard, and pulled it to the side.

Through the steam, I could see blood rush from the wound, mixing with the water and running down the drain. I held a washcloth to the cut, which was more of a flap. Seeing so much blood caused my anxiety to soar; I could

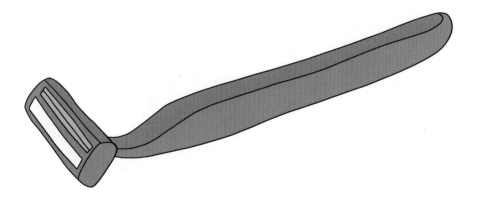

feel my heart beating in my ears, and my vision grew fuzzy. I thought I might pass out.

Turning off the water, I ran from the shower into my mom's office, showing her my bloody shin.

"What happened!?" she asked, rushing to the bathroom to get a Band-Aid.

"I sneezed while shaving," I told her, notorious for my ridiculous sneezes that came in bursts of five to seven.

My mom placed the Band-Aid—the biggest one we had—over the cut and went back to work. Seeing my mom's lack of worry diminished my anxiety, and I suddenly felt only relief, a surge of endorphins pumping through my body. I was no longer numb; instead, I was alive, invigorated and aware, for the first time in months.

It wasn't the first time I'd hurt myself intentionally: I'd punched walls, closed my fingers in desks, run my fingertips along the sharp edges of soda cans. This time was different. All the other times I'd hurt myself, I realized what

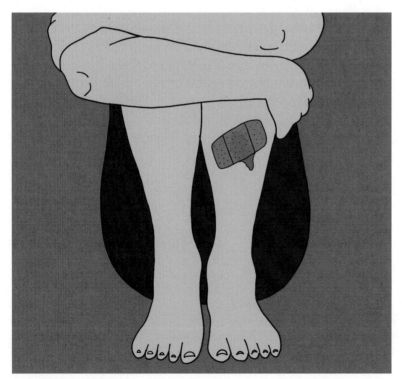

I'd done after the fact–this was the first time I was conscious of what I was about to do before I did it. I had made a choice.

I retreated to my bedroom, and just as quickly as she'd put the Band-Aid on, I tugged it off my wet skin. Pulling the skin open, I marveled at the way I could make the cut "speak" by opening and closing the wound. I liked to watch the blood pool and settle, then begin to trickle again. I liked it so much I got out my camera and began to take photos of my shin, thinking the whole time, *This is the first time I've cut myself*, as if I'd just committed a life-changing act. And though I didn't know it yet, I had.

The next day at school, I showed the cut to anyone who was willing to look at it, telling them the same story I'd told my mom. Showing them that I was hurt seemed like a way of saying *I'm hurting*. No one cared about my leg, thinking it was mildly gross, but it was all I could think about. My brain got stuck on a loop: *Cut cut cut*. Before the end of the day, I asked to be excused to go to the bathroom, took a tack off a bulletin board in the hallway, locked myself in a stall, and scratched three tiny cuts into the top of my wrist.

I was filled with the same anxiety I'd had the night before. Sitting on the toilet, I felt the world was caving in. I was going to die any second from losing such a small amount of blood. I took deep breaths as my vision got blurry, one of the first symptoms I suffer from when I have a panic attack, and put

my head between my knees as my doctor had told me to do. Trying to steady my breathing, I focused on the feeling of my heart pounding, the thumping from where the cuts were, the burning sensation spreading up my arm. When my tunnel vision receded, I looked down at my puffy, swollen wrist and felt reborn. The cuts reminded me I was still capable of feeling something, and I could tell I was falling in love with the rush. I returned to class with my sleeve pulled down, knowing these new cuts couldn't be so easily explained.

For months, my emotions had been cycling from numbness, to unbearable sadness, to intense doom, then back to numbness again. I was hollowed on the inside, like someone had taken a melon baller and emptied me out. My sadness seemed to go on forever and didn't make any logical sense. I had a big group of friends in what was considered the "popular" group of seventh grade, who loved me enough to get to school early to decorate my locker on my birthday. The previous year I would've been ecstatic at this, but this year, I was sure—without proof—that they'd done it out of pity. The things we did together that used to bring me joy—sneaking out at night to wander around our town, getting up early to watch the sun rise over the lake—were dull and uninteresting. As they laughed at jokes that would've once brought me to tears, I barely smiled.

Though on the outside I had a good family life—my parents were together, my sister and I rarely fought, my grandma and I met for lunch once a week—I was a stranger to them, and I felt like I was a burden for merely existing. Sometimes, I'd have flashes of feeling between the stretches of emptiness when I began to wonder how they could bear to love me when I hated myself so much. Then just as quickly as the thought came, it would leave, and I'd be numb again. Nothing was enough to make me feel something, anything at all, until cutting.

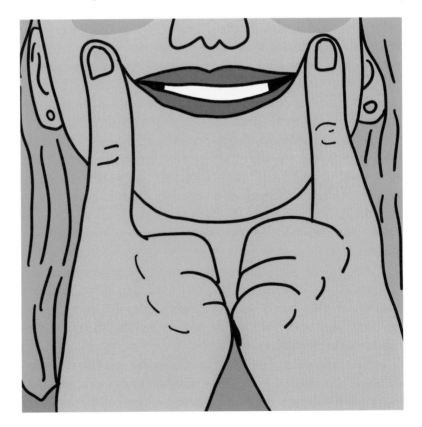

I wanted so badly to tell someone about my discovery, to talk to someone who understood. All my friends seemed effortlessly happy, laughing and smiling, confident in themselves and their actions. I didn't understand what had gone wrong for me to feel so opposite. I was the only person in the world who sat up at night worried she was going to be abandoned by everyone she loved. The only person in the world with a boulder constantly on her chest. I was suffocating. I wanted to know how everyone else seemed to laugh so easily, how they could find joy in such small things. I wanted to know why I couldn't.

That night, I went home and instant-messaged a friend from the year prior who was rumored to be a cutter, and asked her to hang out on Friday. Sarah was an outcast at our school, but popular a few towns over in a group of scene/skater/emo kids. When she eagerly said yes and invited me to join her and her friends at FNS, or Friday Night Skate, that week, a small spark of excitement lit inside me. If Sarah really was a cutter, I guessed her friends were too. I spent the rest of the night trying on different outfits, attempting to find the perfect skinny jean and hoodie combination. I wanted to fit in with this new group in a way I hadn't fit in with my friends for months.

By the time Friday rolled around, the top of my wrist was covered in jagged, small cuts that I hid beneath a pile of friendship bracelets I'd acquired over my many years at summer camp. It was silly and almost perverted to be using this emblem of my innocence to cover my new, non-innocent behavior, and a part of me liked that. I liked that the bracelets on my wrist were a silent way of outing myself as someone who was suffering, a message in a bottle to other cutters. I thought if Sarah saw them, maybe she'd open up to me, and I'd have someone to talk to. Someone who understood not just cutting but the drive toward it.

At her house, as Sarah got ready and tried to decide between wearing black or checkered skinny jeans, I asked her if I could play a song. Always one to obsess, I'd spent my week looking up songs about my new hobby, and found one that resonated with me, "The Way She Feels" by Between the Trees. I wanted to test the waters.

As the song came on, I sat on the floor beside her, watching her do her makeup in front of the mirror behind her door, which was covered in stickers from the local skate shop. The lyrics spoke about cutting; how the deeper one

cuts, things only get worse, and I sang along, trying to see her eyes behind her thick mascara and eyeliner. Though I hoped she'd be moved to confess and tell me the rumors about her were true, she didn't seem to care. When the song ended and began to play again, I walked over to the iHome and took out my iPod, picking at the skin around my nails.

"I really like that song," I said, hoping to start a conversation.

"Yeah, it's good," Sarah said, not giving me much to work with.

"Do you . . . get it?" I asked.

Sarah put down her mascara and walked over to her bed. Reaching underneath, she pulled out a hard-shell pencil case and opened it. Inside were Band-Aids, gauze, Neosporin, razor blades, and a pair of scissors.

"Do you?" she asked, looking into the box expectantly.

"Yeah," I said. "I do."

All the outcasts from the surrounding towns used FNS as a sort of haven, and it was the one place where they, where we, had rule. Though FNS was an ice-skating event, no one cool actually skated. We bought Ring Pops at the snack counter and went to sit in the bleachers of the ice rink, sucking on our sticky fingers and exchanging iPods, listening to new music. I shared "The Way She Feels" and everyone instantly got it, pulling down their bracelets or rolling up their hoodie sleeves and showing how much they'd cut that week. For the first time in months, I felt a

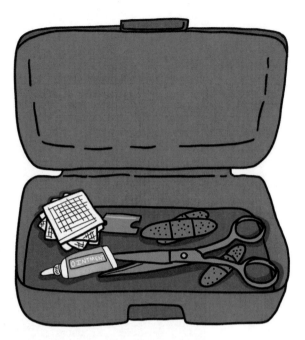

part of something. I pulled back my friendship bracelets and proudly showed off the marks on the top of my wrist as if to say *I belong*. No one judged me, or questioned why I did what I did. We simply sized up one another's sadness from the marks on our bodies, and then migrated outside to watch the boys skateboard.

It was like I'd been part of this group of friends forever, a feeling I'd never had with my friends previously. I was always out of place; not skinny or pretty enough, not cool enough, not, not, not. With these new friends, it seemed we shared these feelings, and because of that, our mutual shortcomings canceled out and we all just accepted one another for who we were. I didn't have to explain to them what sadness felt like, because they felt it too.

These were my people, and soon I was spending all my free time with them. We hung out at the mall for hours every day after school. I anxiously stood outside while they stole earrings from Claire's; we went into Abercrombie and mocked their clothes until we got kicked out, bought packs of jelly bracelets from Hot Topic to hide our cuts, and saw the same horror movies over and over again. Our favorite hangout spot was a gaming center in the basement of the mall, next to a specialty lighter shop. We'd pay by the hour to play

World of Warcraft, drink energy drinks, and spark Zippos while listening to hardcore and screamo. The guys who worked in the shop were older versions of ourselves, and through their existence we had something to look forward to: things wouldn't last forever, one day middle and high school would be over, one day we'd be able to do whatever we wanted. We called ourselves the Crew.

The Crew was made up of around twenty kids spanning across the north suburbs of Chicago, all of us misfits. We had to beg Sarah to eat and Jenny not to throw up her food, constantly try and stop Simon from burning himself, keep David from cutting so deep he needed stitches, beg James not to tattoo Jenny's name on his arm with a tattoo gun he made from an electric toothbrush. Though our problems differed, what we all shared was that we were depressed, and we liked to be around people who made us feel normal.

Each night, no matter how much I'd enjoyed hanging with the Crew, no matter how accepted I'd felt, I'd go home and lock myself in my bathroom with a pair of nail scissors and take them to my wrist. Too anxious to cut in one go, I'd scrape away at my skin until the thin line finally began to bleed, and then I'd move on to the next. But as with the hot water the first time I'd cut, my body got used to the pain, and needed more to feel better. It took five, six, seven cuts to feel the surge I got that first time in only one cut, and the anxiety was duller now.

There was something intoxicating about having someone bear witness to our suffering, and so the Crew put it on display, some more than others. For me, cutting was always a confusing dichotomy between wanting to be seen and not, wanting to be caught but also wanting my behavior to stay a secret forever. I loved feeling something. I loved being the master of my own emotions and body. But most of all, I loved the Crew's begging me to stop while simultaneously telling me it was okay to do what I had to do. I liked feeling attended to, like I mattered, like someone cared that I was hurting.

But it seemed the more I hung around sadness, the sadder I got, and the less I was able to pretend I was anything but miserable. Though I had faked happiness with my old friends, there was no reason to with the Crew. I'd gotten used to being open with my sadness with them, unabashedly sobbing at FNS or the mall, disappearing into a corner to cut. I forgot to hide my feelings, so I walked the halls at school with my head down, my fingers clutched around the sleeves of my shirt. I cried in the library often, or sometimes in the hallway, not caring whether I was seen. Soon my teachers took notice, and started following me into the bathroom, afraid to leave me alone for even a few seconds. When they called home and said they were worried about me, my parents weren't surprised.

My mom had begun to be suspicious of my bracelets, so I'd taken to removing them before bed and draping my arm over my pillow, wrist up, showing her the clean skin and hiding my thighs and the back of my wrist, what was ruined. I cut on the top of my wrist rather than the bottom, partly because I was scared of the thin skin and partly because I believed I could fool adults that way, and so far, it had seemed to work. But when my parents received a phone call from the school stating that they believed I was hurting myself, my nightly show no longer sufficed.

Sitting on my bed, my mom asked me to strip to my underwear and take all my bracelets off. I was terrified of her finding the cuts on the top of my wrist, the line on my ankle, the two small cuts near my hip. But as I took off my clothes, I realized, for the first time, that it was a good thing I wasn't brave enough to cut like my friends did: my cuts looked like accidental scratches. She didn't inquire about the cut on my ankle or any of the others spread randomly across my body. Instead, she asked about the few scabs on my upper arm.

"What are these?" she asked, pointing to a patch of circular cuts where I'd gouged away my skin.

"When I'm anxious, I pick," I said. Ever since I'd had my first panic attack at age nine, my anxiety was something my family knew about and tried to help me manage. And it was true—the cuts were from picking at myself in class, or when I didn't have the opportunity to sneak away and cut, an alternative form of self-harm that was somehow more socially acceptable.

"And this is the reason why everyone's so upset?" she asked.

"I don't know. I'm anxious at school; no one likes me. I walk with my head down, that's probably why people think I'm sad."

"Court, you have to walk with your head high and show those fuckers what you're really about," my dad chimed in from the next room, always fiercely on my side.

"We'll take care of this," my mom said as I got dressed. Then she drove me to Walgreens and picked up Band-Aids, scar cream, and Neosporin.

•

The times I felt most loved was when someone was worried about me, so I gave people reasons to worry. After school one day, my new boyfriend and member of the Crew, Andrew, and I were meandering around town and wandered into a hardware store. When I found a box of razor blades, I picked it up without any true intention of buying it; I was too scared to cut with something so sharp. Not knowing this, Andrew grabbed at the box, trying to put it back on the shelf. I turned my body away from him and took off running down the aisle. Andrew chased me, catching up to me and wrapping his arms around my body, wrestling the box from my hands before setting it down out of my reach. I collapsed and began to sob on the floor, needing more attention than the world was capable of giving.

Like me, Simon felt best when he was in the spotlight. At David's bar mitzvah, he showed up with the sleeve of his white dress shirt soaked in blood. Simon had been threatening suicide for weeks, toying with the Crew's emotions. He would often set his AIM away message to something sinister about him wanting to die, and then skip school the next day and not respond to messages.

His bloodied shirt was a sign that he was serious about his threats, but the Crew saw it as another one of his cries for attention and brushed it off as an annoyingly Simon thing to do. They were frustrated with him and his constant need to be noticed and re-assured, and believed his suicidal impulses were ungenuine, something he was doing only to scare or worry us.

Like Simon, I needed to constantly be coddled, told I was going to be okay, listened to; it was why I'd joined the Crew. Simon and I understood each other, and he was before me on "the chain," which was the system we used to talk each other out of suicide. The idea was: if one of us killed ourself, the person closest to that person would do so next, then the person closest to that person, and eventually, we'd all be gone. If he went, I went. I was in hysterics.

EDIT AWAY MESSAGE ☒

ENTER LABEL: FuUuUcKK IT

ENTER NEW AWAY MESSAGE:

A Ⓐ ʌ A A B I U Link ☺

~* ENDING IT ALL!!!!! SICK of this **SHIT** *** no one luvs me. MoM this is UR FAULT! *~~

Save for later ☐

I'M AWAY   CANCEL

Two friends from the Crew and I got into the elevator of the hotel and rode it to the top floor. I was sobbing, and a general rule in the Crew was never to let a friend having a mental breakdown be alone. We feared for what we'd do if left unattended, and alternated between needing to be taken care of and taking care of one another.

Arriving at the top floor, ten stories up, I stepped out of the elevator and saw that the hotel was designed as a large, open square. The middle of the square was empty, so that one could stare down at the other floors and straight into the lobby. I ran from the elevator and began to hang my upper body off the glass ledge, feeling blood sink into my fingertips and rush to my head in a swan dive. My friends pulled me away, leading me back to the party.

For some reason, it wasn't enough for me to be upset or suicidal; I needed others to see it, be involved in my pain. My friends did their best to help me, but it's hard to stop another's suffering when you're suffering too. I remember sitting in the bleachers of FNS, watching kids skate and thinking about what it was like to be young and happy, complaining to David that my cutting was getting worse and that I felt unlovable and like a burden. He tried to console me, then told me that his cutting was getting worse too. Then he lifted up his T-shirt and revealed a deep heart-shaped cut that he'd carved into his sternum. My cuts, though abundant, were nothing in comparison. As I traced his scabs with my fingers, I switched from needing care to caretaking.

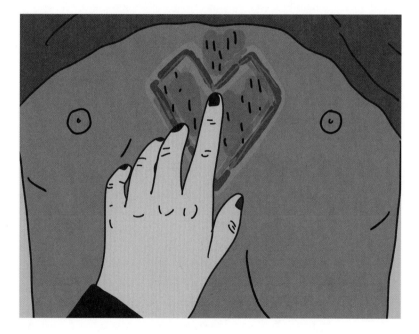

"The chain," I said, reminding him of our pact to stay alive.

"I know," he said, beginning to cry.

"Promise me you'll try," I asked him, not needing to say I meant that he'd try not to kill himself.

"Only if you promise me," he replied.

On a family vacation in Florida, things grew worse. The only thing more trig-gering than being with the Crew was not being with the Crew, and though I was gone just for the weekend, I worried I'd be abandoned by them. When my new-new boyfriend of three days, Anthony, IMed me and told me he hated him-self for dumping his ex-girlfriend for me and that he'd been cutting himself over it, I walked out onto the house's balcony. It was getting chilly outside. I hung my upper body off the railing just as I had at David's bar mitzvah, feeling the blood rush into my forehead and fingertips. As I looked down, I realized that it was a two-story home and I likely would only break a few bones.

Heading into the bathroom, I ran a bath. When it was full, I stripped naked, got into the hot water, and sank beneath it. Opening my eyes and looking up to the distorted ceiling, I exhaled all the air from my lungs and tried to inhale water, but something in my body stopped me. I spurted out of the water, gulping down air, then tried again. This time I closed my eyes, exhaled, and tried to breathe in. Instead I swallowed water, and exited the water coughing, then began to sob. Instead of sinking under again, I just sat in the bath. I went to bed instead of dying, but not before telling all my friends what I'd tried to do.

For Simon, just telling someone about what he'd done wasn't enough; he wanted a witness. When he asked me to video chat with him, the video opened to him slitting his throat from chin to chest. Though the cut wasn't deep, blood ran from it, and I watched as it spread through the fabric of his T-shirt. He smiled, only saying "Ouch" before he began to take Excedrin by the fistful. He swallowed the white pills like they were candy, and then just as quickly as he'd asked me to video chat, he exited from it. I begged him to stay online, to please not go to sleep, to just keep talking to me, to call an ambulance, to get help. I felt that to call for help myself would mean betraying him, and I didn't even know his address. He answered sporadically throughout the night as I sat up waiting for any word from him, telling me he'd thrown up or his stomach hurt.

The next day Simon showed up at school with a shaved head and looking, other than the superficial cut on his neck, no worse for wear. I hugged him as tightly as I could, and he pushed me off him, angry I was making a scene. Before I even had a chance to speak to him, two local policemen trudged into the building and took Simon away to the psychiatric ward.

None of us knew how long he'd be gone, so the Crew started a "Free Simon" Facebook page, where we posted our favorite memories of him. The Crew used what happened to Simon as a warning: stop being so obvious, maybe stop cutting altogether, or you'll be next.

When our parents caught news of Simon's hospitalization, they called for an emergency meeting; it had become clear in the days since he was hospitalized that he wasn't the only one suffering. My parents weren't invited. From what I was told, it was because the rest of the parents believed I was "beyond repair."

I couldn't stop cutting, couldn't stop myself from wanting to die, couldn't stop my sadness. I began to feel afraid of myself, like I wasn't in control of my choices, wasn't the one deciding whether I hurt myself. As I explained this to my friend Katie, she asked if I was ready to stop, to get better, and whether she could call my parents. *Okay*, I wrote back, a sort of half answer. I heard the phone ring and my mom pick up. A few minutes later, she was in my room, asking me to show her my thigh, which was covered in cuts. As I pulled down my sweatpants, I began to sob, realizing my life was about to change and I didn't know yet whether it would be for the better.

"It's going to be okay, Court," she said, going into my closet and taking out a duffel bag. "Were those there last time I checked?"

"Not those, but others," I said, beginning to pack. I knew I was headed for the hospital.

"I didn't know what I was looking for," she said, and then we got in the car.

Not two weeks after Simon was admitted to the psychiatric ward, I found myself at the same hospital, admitted to the same unit. And though he'd stayed for only three days, I wasn't released for week. It seemed that the hospital agreed with the Crew's parents: I was going to be hard to save.

For years, this idea haunted me. The rest of the Crew seemingly healed. Some got therapy, some medication, but most just moved on. Maybe seeing Simon be taken away by the police was enough to put them off their behavior forever. Did they stop just as quickly as they'd started? To me, it seemed that cutting had never mattered to them at all. There was no weaning themselves off, no withdrawal. It was simply something they'd once done, a phase, something they'd gone through. But cutting had taken over my entire life and become an integral part of my being.

I began to frequent the psychiatric hospitals surrounding Chicago, seeking help when I was afraid of myself again. No matter how hard I tried to stop, I somehow always found myself back in a place of hurting myself and wanting to die. Even when I felt better for a bit, the feelings that I was an unlovable burden that everyone wanted to abandon, and the unending emptiness, would always end up creeping back in. Before I was sixteen, I'd been admitted to three separate hospitals and was committed to a residential treatment center in Utah for ten months. With each new admission, each new medication I tried, each new therapist I saw, I was more plagued and confused, left

wondering why I was so different from everyone else in the Crew. Why they could move on, but I was stuck in a Groundhog Day–type loop, years passing by as I continued to feel the same way I had at thirteen.

It wasn't until I was twenty-two–and remembered that during my first hospitalization, the doctors thought I had borderline personality disorder–that I began to do research. When I looked up the symptoms–unstable sense of self, extreme fear of abandonment, impulsive and self-destructive behaviors such as cutting, tumultuous relationships, extreme mood swings, and a pervasive sense of emptiness–I was floored. For the first time, I felt truly seen. Everything began to make sense, and at twenty-three, ten years after my initial hospitalization and that year from hell with the Crew, I was diagnosed.

Upon diagnosis, I was finally able to recognize my behavior as symptoms of my disorder, and make sense of my actions. Having borderline explained my feelings of emptiness, my unsteady sense of self, the way I built my personality around cutting as soon as I began, why I craved attention and felt abandoned when I didn't receive it. I was a textbook case.

For a while, I was angry. Because borderline isn't legally diagnosed until at least age eighteen, owing to the difficulty of separating borderline characteristics from teenage angst and hormones, I suffered through symptoms for years when I could've been learning how to deal with them. It suddenly made sense why no matter how much therapy I got, my symptoms were pervasive as ever: I hadn't been working to heal the core problem I was facing but rather a peripheral effect of it.

I can't help but think that if I had known that around 75 percent of individuals with borderline will attempt suicide; if I had known that 30 percent of borderlines will begin self-harming before age thirteen; if I had known we make up 20 percent of all inpatients in psychiatric wards, perhaps I wouldn't have felt quite so isolated, confused as to why I hurt in a way it seemed no one else I knew did, why it took so much more help to get me to a functional place. Perhaps I wouldn't have succumbed to the cycle of hospitalization after hospitalization at all. Or perhaps it was my fate as someone with borderline, and I was merely fulfilling the stereotypes of my disease.

When I look back at my thirteen-year-old self, I want to hug her. I want to tell her it's going to be okay. That she's going to exist in ten years. That one day, she'll have a diagnosis that explains things. Most of all, I want to tell her that she isn't beyond repair.

Ten Months in Europe

Before La Europa Academy was a residential treatment center for at-risk teen-age girls, it was a bed-and-breakfast, mainly serving newlyweds. Located in Murray, Utah, a suburb situated between Park City and Salt Lake City, La Europa offered convenience and extravagance. As couples pulled up to the tan mansion, they were greeted by two large lion statues, one at each side of the front door, which opened to reveal an entryway featuring a four-tiered, trickling fountain. Each room in La Europa was named after a city in Europe: Munich, Brussels, Helsinki, Barcelona, Budapest. The honeymooners could say they'd spent their week in Dublin, and they wouldn't necessarily be lying. The backyard offered a stone patio, and a pond full of koi ready to be fed. There was a tennis court for lessons, a large pool to swim in during summer. Graced with blue skies an average of 230 days a year and surrounded by towering mountains, La Europa was a dream.

When I arrived at the age of thirteen, La Europa had been converted into a residential treatment center three years prior. The pool had been drained, and it had since gradually filled with dirt and rainwater. The tennis court was cracked, the fountain in the entryway had long been dry, and the pond in the backyard had more browned leaves in it than fish. One thing remained the same: the room names. I moved into Brussels, and joked with the other girls about telling everyone back home that we'd spent the year traveling Europe. But even though none of the couches in the great room matched, the carpets were stained, and the heat didn't work in Munich, La Europa was still beautiful to us. The ceilings were high, so when we laughed, the sound floated through the whole house, and someone was always laughing. The same went for crying, but I remember the laughing more. Guitars lined the walls of the great room and sat in cases under our beds; some of the girls'

voices were so lovely that the world seemed to fall silent when they sang. Every night someone would ask Jennifer or Dani or Lara to perform, and we'd all gather round in awe. Sometimes another girl would play for us, and even though she might not be as talented, we would listen all the same.

La Europa's treatment program was grounded in art therapy, so nearly every wall was covered in art. Next to the bulletin board that had our weekly therapy and school schedule, there were paintings and photographs and drawings. Because La Europa was short on money and didn't have canvas, most of the paintings were done on cardboard, little images of bananas or a brand logo showing through the paint if you looked in a certain light. Even our teachers were artists; the walls in the entryway were lined with portraits of girls who had completed the program that our art teacher, Jane, had lovingly drawn for them as graduation gifts. Looking at them was like some kind of hope: Yes, you were in a treatment center. Yes, you were likely going to be here for a year. Yes, it would be hard. But also: yes, you'd make it out of here, and like those girls on the wall, you'd be happy.

●

I spent the days before I was admitted to La Europa with my parents in a house we rented in the mountains of Park City. We watched movies and my dad made me crepes that were fat like pancakes from the altitude. My mom wrote me a song, recorded it on GarageBand, and sheepishly handed it to me on a CD to listen to when I missed her. Knowing I would be apart from them for months on end, we soaked up our time together by eating our way through Park City's restaurants and exploring the small street fairs that lined the hilly roads. When the time finally came for me to check in, we made the forty-five-minute drive through the winding canyons to Murray. When we pulled into the driveway, my mom turned around from the front seat.

"Don't judge it on the first few days, Court. They follow you around for a while, but it'll get better. You'll love it." Her voice was warm.

I didn't, but it was too late to turn back.

●

After I had been strip-searched, had my belongings checked in, and said good-bye to my parents, I understood what my mom was talking about in the car. I was told that for the first week of my stay I'd be on what was called "safety." On safety you were required to be within five feet of a staff—always "staff," never "staff member"—at all times. You had to eat 100 percent of your food, wait thirty minutes to go to the bathroom after meals, and count out loud as you used the bathroom to ensure you weren't throwing up your food or trying to end your life. A staff was required to watch you shower, you weren't allowed to wear shoes, and when the girls left for events off campus, on safety you were required to stay. I was told that if after a week I hadn't hurt myself, I'd be moved off safety to level one of the program. Then I'd be allowed to start showering alone, wearing shoes, and going off campus, though I'd still have to be in a staff's line of sight at all times and count in the bathroom. Eventually, I'd work my way to level six, gaining privileges as I went, and then I'd be able to graduate and go home.

It was summer, and though I was on safety, it took me a week to fully comprehend the new space I was in. It seemed everything at La Europa was peculiarly similar to the way it was everywhere else. There were friend groups and the worry of where to sit at meals. Girls played *Mario Kart* during free time and took guitar and dance lessons on Sundays. Summer school was a breeze, and on my first day in science class we made baked Alaska to learn about something I've since forgotten, but we cooked it in the same oven we were using to cook our lunch, and it tasted like chicken instead of a sweet dessert. In math class we watched episodes of *Numbers* and discussed the formulas they used to solve crimes.

Though we were all admitted to La Europa because we were suffering from depression and trauma, and the myriad ways they manifest, it seemed everyone was, for the most part, happy. There was a lot of smiling and laughter in a way you wouldn't anticipate at a treatment center. Aside from the two hours a day we spent in group therapy, the three hours a week we spent in individual therapy, and our nightly "community" sessions where we spoke about our goals and what we were struggling with, we were almost normal teenagers. Like normality was within reach.

Becca showed up a week into what would become my ten-month stay. She looked down a lot and was shy in a way that was almost painful, with a voice she purposely made a few octaves higher so she sounded like a child. When Becca moved into Brussels with my roommate, Crystal, and me, we were happy to have someone so sweet living with us. But our happiness quickly turned to frustration after we spent a few nights with her.

At night, whatever had brought Becca to La Europa came out with a vengeance. She kicked and screamed in her sleep, thrashing beneath her royal purple duvet cover. The night staff that monitored us every fifteen minutes would wake her, and she'd have a few minutes of peace before succumbing to her night terrors again. Each morning, the staff would take her to the laundry room and she'd wash her sheets without any explanation. For the first few days, Crystal and I didn't understand, until our room began to reek of urine and a staff set up two fans to constantly try to air out the smell because the windows were permanently locked.

It was customary, when you arrived at La Europa, to share what brought you there during your first night's community meeting. Becca refused to talk for her first three nights, but on the fourth night she spoke up. She told us that she'd been raped daily by the men in her family since she was seven, and that when she was placed in foster care she began to be abused again. She bounced from foster home to foster home until she finally found a loving family that adopted her and sent her to La Europa to make sense of her experiences, and heal. No one knew what to say; I think Becca's trauma was too deep for any of us to process. We looked down and picked at our cuticles and thanked her for sharing, because it was all we could think to do. As soon as she spoke, I felt awful for having been upset about the smell that permeated our room. I was glad I hadn't asked her why she was washing her sheets.

•

Everything at La Europa was routine: Wednesday was breakfast for lunch, Monday dessert night, Sunday night was pizza. We were allowed to shave on Wednesdays and Sundays, supervised by a staff, only with an electric razor, during "hygiene," which was what we called getting ready, and it was scheduled into our day. Every third Friday we went to the Salt Lake City Public Library, which had four stories and huge glass elevators that some girls, including me, were too afraid to ride. The other Fridays we spent volunteering at the soup kitchen or the animal shelter. At every night's community, we each, including staff, went around to talk about what we were working on in therapy, how we were feeling that day, and what our goals were going forward. On Wednesdays, the treatment team met all day to determine which of the girls who'd applied to level up would actually level up, who was up for graduation, and who was receiving a level drop. At any time on a weekday you could be pulled out of what you were doing for individual therapy, on top of group therapy, which was every weekday after lunch. Your therapist decided what groups you were in—eating disorder group, trauma group, anxiety group, addiction group, "sexual reactivity" group; the list of groups offered was long.

On Friday nights, one girl would be allowed to choose where we'd go out to dinner, and her answer was always Chipotle. The staff knew all our names

Schedule

MON	TUES	WEDS	THURS	FRI	SAT	SUN
WAKE UP 6:00 AM	wake up 6:00 AM	wake up 6:00 AM	wake up 6:00 AM	WAKE UP 6:00 AM	wake up 10:00 AM	wake up 10:00 AM
Rec Center	P90X	Rec Center	P90X	yoga	hygiene + breakfast	hygiene + breakfast
hygiene + breakfast	hygiene + breakfast	hygiene + breakfast	hygiene + breakfast	hygiene + breakfast	free time or dance or guitar or piano	deep clean
CLASS 1	CLASS 3	CLASS 1	CLASS 3	Library/volunteering/Field trip		
CLASS 2	CLASS 4	CLASS 2	CLASS 4			
Lunch	Lunch	Breakfast for lunch	Lunch	LUNCH	LUNCH	lunch
electives	electives	electives	electives	electives	study hall + free time	study hall + free time
group therapy	group therapy	group therapy	group therapy	group therapy		
dinner	dinner	dinner	dinner	dinner	dinner off campus	pizza for dinner
Free time	free time	Study hall	Free time	Free time	movie night	AA or Reflection
Study hall	study hall	rec night	study hall	study hall		
Community	community	Community	community	Community	community	community
hygiene	hygiene	hygiene	hygiene	hygiene	hygiene	hygiene
10:00 PM Lights out	10:00 PM Lights out	10:00 PM Lights out	10:00 PM Lights out	10:00 PM Lights out	10:00 PM Lights out	10:00 PM Lights out

and orders by heart and to expect us at six thirty sharp every Friday night. On Saturdays, we screened an approved movie that was PG-13 or under, all gathering around to watch it on an old box TV. Sunday mornings we'd wake up and deep-clean our house for three hours or as long as it took us, do homework, then have pizza for dinner, after which some girls would go to Alcoholics Anonymous while others of us had a two-hour period called "reflection," where we were allowed only to journal or sit silently in our beds or read. Then we'd have hygiene, and go to sleep.

Because everything was routine, tiny things meant the world to us, like calling "shotty" before a car ride. Sitting in the front seat of what we called the "treatment vans," the huge white vans with tinted-black windows that seated fourteen and transported us everywhere, was a huge privilege. This was not only because we had to be above level three in order to do so but also because the girl who sat up front got to choose the music for the entirety of the ride.

Getting shotty for the ride to the rec center on Monday and Wednesday mornings didn't mean much—the ride was less than ten minutes. But on

COURTNEY'S MIX!

1. Check Yes Juliet
   - We the Kings
2. Feel Good INC.
   - Gorillaz
3. Hero/Heroine
   - Boys Like Girls
4. BIGCITYDREAMS
   - Never Shout Never!
5. INTO YOUR ARMS
   - The Maine
6. Ocean Avenue
   - Yellowcard
7. Dare 4Distance
   - Never Shout Never!
8. Dear Maria, count me in
   - ALL TIME LOW
9. IF it means a lot to you
   - A Day To Remember

APPROVED BY DEVON 1/12/10
*ANYONE CAN LISTEN

the nights we drove to the canyons to roast pink Starbursts and marsh-mallows over a fire while we held community, or to the Jamba Juice and Nickelcade, when the ride was twenty minutes or more, sitting shotty was heaven. Though every CD we burned on our home passes to bring back for the car rides had to be approved by the staff song by song, and our radio choices could be vetoed at any moment if they so much as swore, in a place where everything we did was monitored, the freedom to choose music in the car was as close to true freedom as we could get.

The Nickelcade was a cheesy arcade filled with Skee-Ball, Whac-a-Mole, and every other arcade game one could think of, and each game cost only a nickel. We weren't allowed to play the games that had guns, but otherwise, the Nickelcade was ours to conquer. For girls who lived in a treatment center without access to cell phones, iPods, or even the Internet, a game of pinball felt like magic.

We were each allotted five dollars in nickels and could choose whatever prize we could pay for with the tickets we earned. There was no saving your nickels for the next rec night—no one was allowed to have money at La Europa. Money was a flight risk, which staff spent immeasurable time trying to minimize, so much so that every piece of clothing we had was inventoried and we were allowed only a select number of clothes in each category. In the morning when we got dressed the staff in charge of us that day would mark down what we were wearing in our chart. That way, if we ran away, they'd know what to tell the police: "She was wearing a blue shirt with red stripes and black jeans. Green socks, gray UGGs with the fur turned down. A black zip-up sweatshirt, unzipped, Officer."

After we spent an hour toying with joysticks, playing air hockey, and trying to hit the jackpot on every game we played, we'd gather around the glass countertop of the prize area holding on to our receipt from the ticket counter and survey what we could afford. Most of us would walk out with a key chain even though we weren't allowed to own bags to hang them on because of the flight risk, or a handful of Laffy Taffy and a Tootsie Roll. It didn't matter that the prizes were lame. It just felt good to get outside the walls of La Europa, for a while.

We'd load into the treatment vans and drive home, where we'd pile out of the cars and line up by the door, ready to be checked in. Forming three lines in the entryway next to the fountain, we'd wait to be patted down by one of the staff. The illusion of normalcy we'd had while we were out would shatter.

They had to make sure we weren't hoarding our nickels, as if nickels could've gotten us anywhere. We all knew we were trapped, whether we liked it or not, in Murray, Utah, until we graduated or our insurance ran out and our parents couldn't pay the hefty price to help us get better anymore.

•

Usually at least one girl out of our group of thirty-two would have a breakdown each day, and at any given moment at La Europa you could almost guarantee that someone in the house was crying. Group therapy was usually hard; some girl would speak and unintentionally trigger another. There were often days that marked a year since a girl had been raped, or had had to have an abortion; there were the one-month marks of sobriety for girls addicted to meth who yearned for it all the time. But some days, there was a lull in the sadness in the house: Every girl who applied to level up would have her request granted by the treatment team, no one would cry in group therapy, home passes would be approved. Community lasted only a few minutes while everyone spoke about how they were doing well.

If the energy in the house was good, your therapist might be extra nice to you and take you to Stop & Shop to get you a candy bar or decaffeinated soda before therapy, or let you have therapy in a park somewhere if it was sunny out. Sometimes the staff would feel stir-crazy and let us walk down the road to Wheeler Farm and pet the pigs and horses and shoo flies off the cows and take pictures in the hay. Or if the budget had been increased recently, we'd be allowed extra treats on rec night and could walk to Woody's, a drive-in diner down the street, to pick up grasshopper milkshakes. During those days, I wondered if we were as broken as we seemed, or if we'd just had a lot of bad days that were strung together in a long row and we were finally out of the woods.

Other days, everything went wrong, and if one girl started crying, then everyone would start to cry with her. Sometimes we were ushered to our rooms quickly and without explanation, told that we were to stay in our beds and read or journal and be absolutely silent until further notice.

The first time this happened to me, I remember how Eden's screams could be heard in every room of the house. Our great room had two-story ceilings, with a walkway halfway up that connected the second floor and overlooked both the great room and the kitchen. Eden was crumpled on one of the green suede couches, her body heaving with sobs. Four staff surrounded her, ready to put her in a hold if necessary. Until Eden's situation was fixed, or she was taken to a hospital to be sedated, we all were to remain in our beds. None of us knew what had made Eden so upset, so upset, but we knew what had brought her here. We all had a story; Eden's was that she'd taken a nail and hammered it into her leg down to the bone. The hole never healed and was always leaking, like a faucet that never fully shut off.

It seemed most of the staff had just as little information as we did. As we sat in our beds, fidgeting with both anxiety and boredom, they texted on their Nokia phones with impressive speed. I always wondered what they were saying, but on that day my curiosity felt urgent.

After two hours of mindless journaling and wishing I'd checked out another book from the library when we'd gone two weeks before, the staff watching us, Charlotte, stood up.

"We can have dinner now."

And like that, it was over. Eden was escorted to her room by two staff. We didn't know what she'd done then, but later we found out that a blade from her eyeliner sharpener had gone missing from the "sharps closet," where the staff secured items they deemed dangerous. For the next twenty-four hours she'd sit in her bed on shutdown, the level of our program below even safety. Shutdown was La Europa hell.

As Eden went up to her room, the rest of us went downstairs for dinner. We gathered at our giant table and ate the horrible fried tofu our chef, Carissa, had made. We laughed and joked and told stories too loudly, happy to be able to talk again. Even though we were in treatment, even though we all suffered from depression and anxiety and so many of us

had been raped and some of us had tried to kill ourselves and most of us cut ourselves when we were sad, we were happy. For that moment, at least, everyone was but Eden. And hopefully, one day, that happiness would last forever.

•

The girls at La Europa were always replacing one another; as one girl would graduate, another would be admitted. The girls I met when I first arrived were not the girls who were there when I left, and the personality of the house morphed depending on who was there at the time. That house was always changing, but it seemed to hold on to those who had been there before. The air in La Europa felt different from the air elsewhere, aged in a way. Like it knew something that we'd have to stay there to learn.

I often wonder what it would have been like to go to La Europa when it wasn't a treatment center, but that period in the house's history seems too painful to picture. I don't want to imagine the fence in the backyard stripped of all its handprints, the handprints of girls who had graduated but wanted to leave their mark on the place that healed them. La Europa, the rec center, our schoolhouse, Woody's, Wheeler Farm, the canyons, Chipotle, the Nickelcade, Murray, Utah. I don't want to imagine a time when the house, and the world around it, was perceived as happier than it was when I was there, because I didn't, and still don't, believe there is a possibility of a place more beautiful.

HOW SUGARY CEREAL KEEPS ME ALIVE:

1. I realized sugary cereal is magic my first time in a psychiatric ward. In that moment, Fruity Pebbles transported me to a world where I hadn't tried to drown myself, one where things were too pure for 13-year-olds like me to want to die. Amid the beige walls and meals of vanilla pudding, even the box appeared like a firework.

2. In ways, cereal is better than therapy — this is because therapy is real and practical and hard work and cereal is magic! Cereal, for just a moment, is a cure-all, instant happiness in a box, a flavorful reminder of all that's beautiful and worth existing for in the world. In the words of Tony the Tiger, It's grrreat!

3. I could likely trace the calming effects of a heaping bowl of cereal to dialectical behavior therapy (DBT), an offshoot of cognitive behavior therapy (CBT), created in the '80s to better treat borderline. DBT encourages mindfulness, requiring patients to observe, describe, participate in order to manage symptoms of anxiety. Truth be told, I despise DBT, but time and time again, when I am at my lowest, I find myself pouring a bowl of cereal and investing myself in its flavors and the mere sight of it like my life depends on it. And in a way, it does.

4. On the days when borderline makes me feel like I have nothing to get out of bed for, I dream about the first bite of Lucky Charms with the perfect marshmallow-to-regular-piece ratio, saturated with just the right amount of oat milk. I picture the bright colors of the box and the reminder of luck and rainbows, and I get myself out of bed. I remind myself things may hurt but they won't kill me. I remember things aren't all shitty, people do love me, that to eat something so pure is for it to become part of me too, even if just for a moment.

A Marvel

When my dad was sick and on the verge of dying, I wanted to join the circus. It seemed like a place I'd belong; somewhere I wouldn't be a freak show.

When I pictured the main attractions, I wanted my pain to be as visible as theirs, for strangers on the street to understand that a part of me was missing.

The closest I got to the circus was art high school, and in a lot of ways, they felt like one and the same. The academy was composed of six departments (music, theater, musical theater, visual art, dance, and media art), populated by 120 students, and felt like a departure from the real world. A teacher once told me how he lost his virginity; one let me feel her hair when Accutane had stopped it from producing oil and she hadn't washed it in nine days. Friends and I went to smoke cigarettes at rickety picnic tables by a set of abandoned train tracks at lunch, returning for our art classes in the afternoon happy and excited to be among family.

We were a motley crew guided by older versions of ourselves. An English teacher with no certificate and a degree in radio introduced us to Gabriel García Márquez. Sometimes, we called our teachers "Mom" and "Dad."

I was a member of the media arts department. Media housed animators, writers, and filmmakers, and we were known as the assholes of the school. Our media teachers weren't shy about telling us that their art forms were superior to all the others, and though we didn't have the bodies of the dancers or the fame of the actors, we believed them. Our "us versus them" mentality kept us from winning the yearly school-wide pumpkin-carving competition but bonded us together fiercely. When my dad was sick, media was the first to know.

My dad had been diagnosed with diverticulitis when I was in third grade. I have just a few memories: how he suddenly doubled over in pain, the subsequent hospital visits, the diagnosis, the way he then couldn't eat popcorn or fruit with seeds and needed two seedless bottom buns when he ate hamburgers. I was young and couldn't comprehend the intensity of his pain, or the way it must have felt to have two young daughters and be told that you had an incurable disease that was typically seen in men much older than you.

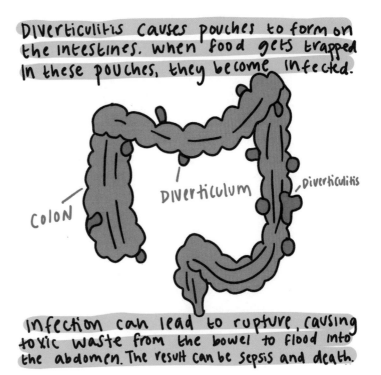

Diverticulitis causes pouches to form on the intestines. when food gets trapped in these pouches, they become infected.

COLON

Diverticulum

Diverticulitis

Infection can lead to rupture, causing toxic waste from the bowel to flood into the abdomen. The result can be sepsis and death.

He had already been in and out of the hospital most of my life, suffering from back pain so intense that it once paralyzed him as he read me a bedtime story and left him immobile in my bed for a day and a half. I remember him walking with a glossy cane after he finally had surgery to fix the herniated spinal disk, and the way I watched the machines wrapped around his calves inflate and deflate when he was in the hospital. But the

scar that ran down his lower back faded beneath his freckles and wispy orange hair, the same way the rest of his scars had.

Though he'd always been sick or injured in one way or another, he never acted ill. He once lived months with a broken wrist before getting it checked out, which necessitated surgery and the insertion of pins that stuck out of his arm for weeks. When he shattered his patella, which then shredded the surrounding tendons, the surgery that followed allowed him to use accessible parking spaces for six months. Rather than talk about his pain, he played the injury off as something exciting, boasting about the parking space whenever we drove together. When diverticulitis was added to his list of ailments, for a long time it seemed like nothing had changed other than a new pill bottle taking up space in our medicine cabinet.

He took the pills quietly, like–he believed–a man.

•

It was early October and he was in the hospital for what felt like the hundredth time that year. During first period I'd gotten the text from my mom I'd come to dread—*Girls, don't worry, but Dad's in the hospital again*—and passed through the rest of my classes a ghost of who I'd been when I got out of bed in the morning.

Knowing my dad's distaste for doctors, I understood that his pain must've been unbearable, which rendered my mom's assurance that we need not worry unconvincing at best. I felt a sort of phantom hurt at the thought of losing him, and also because part of him was already gone. I knew I'd return home to a quiet house with casseroles and flowers taking up the space he usually occupied.

During a fifteen-minute break, I walked to the CVS across the street from school. While I usually came to buy candy or notecards, I headed that day to the greeting card aisle. Scanning the Get Well Soon section, I opened card after cheesy card.

I just wanted something that would make him laugh.

Back at school, we sat with our desks in a large half circle, the head of our department wearing his signature purple velvet blazer at a larger desk in front of us. Each afternoon, he made announcements to the whole department before the filmmakers headed to film aesthetics and we writers to poetry class or workshop. Before he started to speak, I raised my hand.

"My dad is sick again. I bought him a card–I'd really appreciate if you all would sign it." I passed the card to my right. Helen, a small girl who dressed like a businesswoman and always wore kitten heels, began to sign it in her elegant cursive.

Mr. R, who served as the "dad" of media arts, spoke up: "Why can't you just write your own?" He sort of laughed, then looked around and made a gesture with his hands as if he was saying, *C'mon*.

The room fell quiet, all side conversations stopping abruptly. This was the third card they'd seen since August, and to make matters worse, I had transferred to the academy as a sophomore; we were now just a month into school. I must've taken the notion of us being a family to heart too quickly, done the borderline thing and fallen into idolization instead of taking the time to build true connections, forgotten that I was an adopted addition still discovering where I belonged.

I felt my face grow hot. Helen had finished signing, and I wanted to snatch the card from the hand of the person now holding it, to run to the train tracks or maybe get on a train and ride it to Wisconsin, the west suburbs, anywhere far from the fake family I spent my days with and the empty home I'd return to that night. I opened my mouth to protest but didn't say a thing. It was too painful to tell him that I thought if enough people wanted my dad to live, he would.

Mr. R taught our fiction classes. Maybe he was used to recognizing stories– even the ones we tell ourselves.

•

I'd met Layla at the beginning of August. She was going into her junior year at the academy and was the ex-girlfriend of a boy I knew from a math class I'd taken at my former school. If the academy felt far from the real world, Layla felt like going to space. She was a contortionist and trapeze

● LAYLA

JULY 28th, 2011

has anyone ever told you you look like Stevie Nicks??? 😊😊😊

can i take you out? Evanston, Jamba Juice?

I've gotten that a few times! and I'd luv to 💕💕💕

📷 ODD ⋯

artist, sometimes dabbling in aerial silks and clowning. She'd grown up in a world I thought existed only in books and movies. Her father was a traveling magician and her mom his lovely assistant, and I was fifteen with a dying dad and in desperate need of an escape.

When she first messaged me, I was ecstatic. We met up a few weeks later, on a hot day when it was drizzling slightly, and walked to a back-alley bookstore that had a parrot that talked when you entered. Layla was excitable and serious and had hair like a mane that seemed to make up most of her body, which stood under five feet tall. She was preparing to apply to a prestigious circus school in Montreal, spending her time either at the gym practicing her contortion with her coach, or working with our French teacher, whom we called Madame, trying to master the language. I didn't know whether I loved her or found her fascinating, or both, but two weeks later we were dating.

It was Friday, only a few days since my dad was admitted to the hospital, and as much as I wanted to go home and help my mom in any way I could–vacuuming, assisting my younger sister with homework–I was scared to be in my house. I couldn't stand being there without my dad, not knowing when he'd be home again, or if he'd return at all. The lack of him filled the entire space and made me feel suffocated, so instead, I went to Layla's, promising

myself I'd visit the hospital and give him the partially signed card the next morning.

The two of us lay on the couch in her living room, our legs entangled. A movie droned on in the background, a dumb romantic comedy I'd never seen before that Layla found hilarious. I couldn't pay attention. I focused instead on the waffles we'd made for dinner, using the waffle maker I'd gifted Layla for her birthday. They were shaped like circus animals.

On the box the images were clear, but once batter was poured into the molds and cooked, the shapes became puffier, hard to distinguish. I held what I thought was a juggling monkey in my hand, though it looked more like a Rorschach inkblot. I took a bite.

"Do you want to go upstairs?" I asked Layla, muting the TV. "I think your parents are probably asleep by now."

She smiled in response, taking my hand and dragging me off the couch so that we could run to her bedroom: a small room with high ceilings, in which her dad had recently rigged a trapeze. It was all we could talk about. Layla was excited that she would have more time to practice her routines, as she was hoping to get her GED soon and enroll in the Montreal circus school in the coming year. I liked feeling as though we had our own personal playground, a place where I could hang and swing like an unencumbered kid.

Once in her room, Layla changed into a leotard while I wished she'd stay in the in-between phase where she was naked and couldn't yet choose what to wear. There was such magic in her movements that I didn't want anything, no matter how small, to be obscured by fabric.

"Want to see a routine I've been working on?" Layla said. "No one's seen it yet."

"Ooh, aren't I lucky," I teased as she queued up the music, instructing me to press Play once she was in position.

As the music began she lay on her stomach. She swung her legs over her shoulders from behind so that she was sitting on her own head, then pushed up so she was supporting herself only with her arms, her feet dangling over her face. Easing back to the floor, she unrolled herself and stood up, placing her hands on the trapeze and twirling around the bar until she held herself above it, then swung around once more to take a seat on the top.

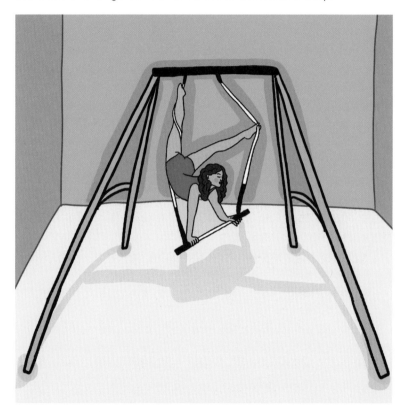

As she hung from it and contorted into different positions, then uncoiled once again, I couldn't stop thinking about my dad. I pictured his colon twisting in on itself, sprouting inflamed polyps from places that were once smooth. I wondered if it hurt her to move like this, if my dad was sleeping or hurting or if the morphine was working. Finally, when I felt I could interrupt, I walked over to Layla and placed my hands on the bar, feeling the rough white tape beneath my palms before moving them to the soft skin of her thighs.

My dad was released from the hospital in the morning. When I walked through the doorway, I ran to hug him, reminding myself to be gentle. When I was in his arms, though, he hugged me tight, so I squeezed back. At once, life resumed normalcy.

•

"You sure you're okay, Dad?" I said as we pulled up to the train station before school. He'd been out of the hospital for a week, and though he had seemed to be improving when they released him, he hadn't made any progress since. Still, each morning, noon, and night he diligently took his medication, waiting for the pain in his stomach to recede and his energy to come back.

"I'm fine," he croaked, wincing as he spoke, then forced a smile. "I love you, Bear Bear."

I opened my car door, unsure of what more I could do. "Can I see?" I asked before getting out of the car.

He opened his mouth, exposing weeping yellow sores that lined his tongue and throat. He grimaced as he did. A few spots were bleeding.

"My medicine should begin working soon," he assured me. "Now get over there, you don't want to miss your train."

"Love you," I said, closing the door, and through the window I saw him mouth that he loved me too.

My phone buzzed with a text from my mom: *I'll be a phone call away if you need me.* She and my sister were on their way to London for the weekend, and my dad had assured them he was fine to take care of himself while they were gone–after all, it was only a few days, and I'd be with him.

Life had felt like it'd come to a stall each time he was admitted to the hospital, and I think London came as a breath of fresh, foggy air.

The day passed slowly, a crawl. After having seen those sores, I kept expecting a text from my dad saying he was on his way to the hospital, or at least the doctor, but a text never came. I didn't make the mistake of telling media arts he was still sick. Instead, I concentrated on the party Layla was hosting after school, a good distraction. When the bell finally rang, it seemed like half the academy hailed and crammed into cabs headed to her house.

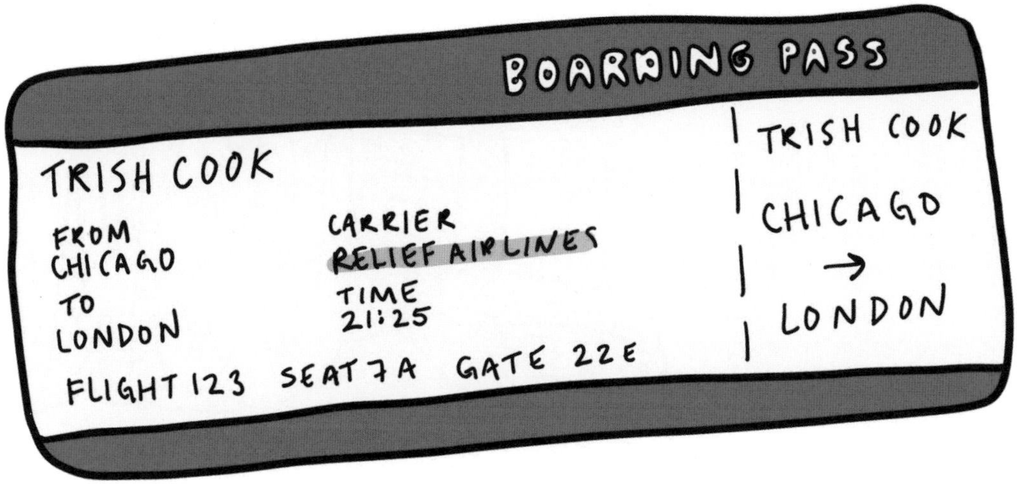

BOARDING PASS

TRISH COOK

FROM
CHICAGO
TO
LONDON

CARRIER
RELIEF AIRLINES

TIME
21:25

FLIGHT 123   SEAT 7A   GATE 22E

TRISH COOK

CHICAGO
→
LONDON

Each year since the nineties, the academy had put on a showcase called the AIDS Benefit, which donated all its profits to those whose bodies were failing them. The visual artists created work to be sold in the gallery before the show, then gathered with the rest of the audience and watched the other departments perform. It was a sort of magnificent talent show presented by people who would later study at Juilliard or be on Broadway, in MoMA. Those of us who weren't performing were going to Layla's to help bake cupcakes that would be sold beforehand.

We danced around the kitchen, eating batter and making up routines on the spot. All of us laughed. I felt, for a moment, like I didn't have anything to worry about.

Layla wrapped her hands around my waist as I spooned red velvet batter into cupcake liners, nuzzling her head into my neck.

"Stay later," she said.

I glanced at the clock, knowing that in order to make my train I'd have to leave for the station soon.

My dad was alone and expecting me, but I dialed his number and waited for him to pick up the phone.

"Do you mind if I take the next train instead?" I asked him once he answered. "We still have a lot of baking to do."

"I can't stay up that long, Courtie," he replied. I could hear the defeat in his voice, which was still coming out raspy and strained. "I'm sorry."

I'd seen his mouth that morning and knew his stomach was still shot with pain—how could I have even asked?

•

I laid my head against the train window the whole ride home. When the train came to my stop forty-five minutes later, I almost ran to the car.

When I opened the door, I asked him to show me his mouth again. The blisters that were there that morning had multiplied and spread like wildfire, his tongue swelling. He told me he hadn't drunk water or eaten in a day, that to do so would set his mouth ablaze. He hadn't even been swallowing his spit he was in so much pain. I asked him again if he was taking his medication, and even though he was, looking at his mouth made it seem otherwise.

When we got home, he crawled into bed and I sat up in mine. I could hear him struggling to breathe, his inhales and exhales coming in labored, erratic spurts. The entire situation felt too big for my fifteen-year-old self, too much to bear. So I did what I could, which was to get him water and put on a brave face.

Filling a plastic cup with ice water and placing a straw into the drink, I walked from the kitchen to his bedroom.

"Why don't we try to take a few sips?" I asked, my voice fake and cheerful.

"Can't, Court. Thanks for bringing it. I'll try later," he wheezed.

"I really think you should go to the hospital." I tried not to sound desperate.

"I'm taking my meds. Don't worry about me."

"I really think—"

"I said don't worry. Good night, Courtie." When he finished speaking, he turned over so he wasn't facing the water, which I'm sure he felt was taunting him.

Slinking back to my room, I positioned myself close to the wall our bedrooms shared and listened to his breathing. Every time it seemed he was breathing well for a bit, the silence between his breaths stretched longer and longer until a pained wheeze would surface from the quiet. Sitting on my bed, I tried to cry quietly enough that I could still hear the wheezes. I felt helpless, and even though I drank on Friday nights, had sex on the weekends, and often thought being fifteen was a sort of adulthood, in that moment I felt I had aged backward and become a child.

I took out my computer and FaceTimed Layla, erupting into tears as soon as she answered.

"What's wrong, baby?" she said, concern in her brown eyes.

I think he's dying, I wrote back, unable to choke out words between my sobs.

"All right, you need to call your mom," she said, her voice stern in the way it got when she was directing a show, or was angry with me.

I'd tried to keep my mom and my sister updated with texts, but it was hard to articulate the magnitude of my fear. I had said that he was "really struggling" and had a "blistered tongue," but there was no way for me to text about how bad it truly was–it just didn't come across in words. I knew if I was able to articulate how awfully he was doing, my mom would be on the next flight home, and I didn't want to break my dad's trust or ruin my sister and mom's trip. More than anything, I was afraid.

But Layla's words had shaken me into action; I think I had to hear the word "dead" from someone other than myself for it to become real. It gave me the courage to call my mom, even though it was six in the morning and it had taken me all night to convince myself to do so and I didn't even know if she had service away from the hotel in London.

When my mom answered the phone, I started to wail. "Dad needs to go to the hospital but won't," I said. "*I think he's dying.* I don't say that to scare you, but I really think he's dying. His tongue is lined with these yellow blisters and he hasn't eaten and can't drink and he's wheezing–"

"I'll handle it. Get ready for school. Thanks, Court," she said, and hung up the phone. Her voice was caring but rushed, and I could tell she was about to call him, furious.

As she and my sister cried in the London Eye, my mom called my dad's doctor, who said he needed to go to the hospital immediately. I got ready for school and didn't let him know about my phone call. As he dropped me off at the train station, we played the same game: I asked him to go see a doctor, he showed me his tongue and refused, I hugged him goodbye. At school, I tried to take notes and see from behind my swollen eyes. He drove to work and wheezed at his desk until my mom called and berated him for not taking control of his health. She was livid that he'd put me in the position I was in, and begged him to go to the hospital. He was too stubborn or afraid to admit something was seriously wrong, but said he'd go at lunch just to appease her. She had to trust his word, as she was about to get on an eight-hour flight home without any way of knowing whether he would follow through.

When my dad finally went to the hospital, we learned he had become allergic to the medication that was supposed to be calming his episode of diverticulitis, which had caused sores and blisters to form all the way from his stomach to his mouth. Three of the polyps on his colon had burst, leaking toxic waste into his abdomen, something that's usually fatal. I really had been listening to the sounds of him dying through my bedroom wall.

•

My mom and sister were home within a day, and never had I been so grateful not to be alone. Each time I closed my eyes, I could still see his fat yellow tongue and hear his labored breathing. I wanted to lie in bed for a while, to be taken care of, to shed myself of that fear.

But I couldn't ask to be taken care of when my dad still had so far to go before he was healthy. Instead, I went to the AIDS Benefit. Surrounded by Layla and the media arts department and everyone else who had taken over my red velvet cupcake duties when I went home to care for my dad, I sold baked goods and worked the cash register. When the lights began to flicker and the performers headed backstage, I took a seat on the floor in front of the first row, my ear placed directly beside the speakers. When a singer belted a note, I felt something inside me quake. As I watched the dancers, I felt the beat in my body the way they felt it in theirs. I was aware of myself, and I wanted to feel the way my body worked, the way it put itself together.

When it was Layla's time to perform, I watched her bend and fold, noting the differences between the way she looked under the bright lights versus the dimness of her bedroom. I felt the ways her muscles tensed. Layla contorted into unfathomable shapes, and just when we all feared she'd break, she'd un-wind herself again. I cried thinking about bodies and their ability to transform.

The next morning, I went to visit my dad. He lay in the hospital bed, so freckled and stubborn and fiery red and beautiful. I brought him a card signed only by me, and watched as he took a sip of water without wincing. Then he stuck out his tongue at me, and I marveled at the pink of it.

Your Body Is a Temple

I call the boy who has broken my heart continually over the past two years. My hands are shaking because I'm scared he won't answer and even more scared that he will. I don't know what I want to say, but I know that whatever it is, he's the one I want to say it to. Donald Trump has just been named the president-elect, it's two thirty in the morning, and I've had five glasses of red wine. I'm tired and something inside me is aching. Four hours ago, this was an outcome I couldn't have dreamed of. I had a tattoo planned for when Hillary became our first female president: the Venus symbol beneath my left breast. Now, this night feels godless.

Listening to the phone ring, I look over at my best friend asleep on the couch, so peaceful and unaware of the new world we're entering. I think of the Shakespeare quote: "Hell is empty, and all the devils are here." I hope she sleeps on that couch until morning. I hope she can push off this pain for another few hours.

The boy answers and I ask him to come over, tell him that I need someone to hold me. We haven't spoken in eight months but without hesitation he agrees, says he'll be right there. I don't know what I'm doing. I think the real reason I invited him over is that I'm hurting and I want to control my hurt. I know exactly the way he hurts me every time, and I'm opening the door. But I rationalize that in a world so filled with disappointment, a world where a presidential candidate who ran entirely on a campaign of fear and hatred got elected, I need to shed myself of the anger and dislike I have for those who have wronged me. So, I am starting at the source: the boy who has caused me the most pain.

I go to my room and I put on Bright Eyes, who sing that love is an excuse to hurt yourself and others. I stare at my ceiling. *Hurt me*.

•

We spoon all night. I am comforted by his touch and the way he pulls me back toward him if I begin to inch away. A friend of ours was assaulted a few days ago in Hell's Kitchen for being gay; five men attacked him and left him with a broken orbital bone and wrist. We are afraid of hearing more of these stories, of having to watch more friends suffer. I think that the only things good right now are the way he's holding me, his familiar smell of cologne and cigarettes. I don't think I believe in God, but I know I feel something holy when someone I love holds me. This is my church. The last thing I see before I fall asleep is the bottle of champagne I bought earlier in the day to celebrate.

When I wake up, he asks me how I'm feeling. I check my phone and have over ten texts from people who care about me, telling me how sorry they are about Trump's victory, my loss. I think that everyone knows this feels like a death to me. I look at the boy. He's leaving for class and I am afraid to be alone. I tell him I'm going to go talk to a God I'm unsure even exists.

I put on a sweatshirt and walk three blocks to a church that has large signs hanging from its stone exterior that say everyone is welcome there. When I go to open the wooden doors, they're locked, so I sit on the steps outside and hope that just being near a church will bring me some clarity. I want answers as to why the world is the way that it is, but if I can't get answers, I want peace.

When sitting outside doesn't seem like enough, I call the church's number and ask whether they're open at all during weekdays. The woman who answers has a soft voice and tells me that the church is closed, but their chapel is open every day from nine to four for private meditation. I thank her, then walk around the building and try every single door until I find one that's unlocked.

The chapel is small and empty. There's an altar at the front, a bowl of holy water that reminds me of a birdbath, and four wooden pews on each side of the room. I sit down in one of them, take off my backpack, and bow my head. I don't know how to do this: how to go to church, how to pray. This isn't something I'm familiar with, something I do or have ever done. I didn't grow up going to church—I can probably count how many times I've been to Mass on one hand. But we all turn to something when we're hurting. Sometimes it's sleeping or drinking a bottle of wine. Sometimes it's calling the boy who broke your heart to hold you for a night. Sometimes it's God.

I don't know if you can hear me, or if you can that you're listening, or if you exist at all. If you do, I'm sorry for saying you don't, and if you do, I don't understand why you'd let this happen. I want to believe the world is inherently good. I want to believe in you and your boundless acceptance and forgiveness, but all I feel right now is anger. I want to ask you for a sign this is going to get better, or for you to give me strength, but I don't want to ask for that. I want to have strength innately, all from myself.

There's a lot more I could say, but I hear the door open. A woman in a gray tweed skirt, black blazer, and leather flats enters the chapel. She makes it half-way down the aisle before bowing and making the sign of the cross, then sits down and bows her head, closing her eyes. Suddenly, I feel out of place and silly for even coming here. I feel underdressed in my sweatshirt and leggings and like I somehow was disrespectful for not going through the motions as she just did. The church is stuffy and hot and musty and closing in on me. I pick up my backpack and head out.

•

When I studied abroad in Florence, I took a weekend trip to Rome. On the third Sunday of the month, when entrance to the Vatican was free, my friends and I boarded the metro. When the doors opened at the station closest to

Vatican City, everyone began to run. I didn't know what we were running toward or away from, but I followed the crowd, weaving around children and street vendors and pigeons along the cobblestone road while trying not to lose my friends. When young men and old women alike began to jump over fences and scale stone pillars, I followed suit. It wasn't until I heard a booming yet comforting voice beginning to pray in Italian that I realized I was about to see the pope give a sermon.

Surrounded by nuns, priests, and locals, I bowed my head in sync with their movements, wiped my brow under the hot sun. The nuns, who had likely seen the pope give sermons dozens of times, looked as wowed by his presence as I was. I knew they felt it too: the waves of emotion, crashing over all of us. I thought about how, the night before, I had been drinking and doing cocaine off a toilet seat in a hostel bar. But here, the next morning, I was in the presence of the closest person to God and all his believers.

When the pope left the balcony he had spoken on, and people started to mill outside the courtyard we'd gathered in, I entered Saint Peter's Basilica. As soon as I made my way inside, I fell to my knees and began sobbing.

I knew instantly that I'd never be in a place so beautiful ever again. Looking at the ornate sculptures and paintings, the painstaking effort and craftsmanship that went into every detail of their creation, I understood for the first time what people meant when they spoke about the glory of God.

Before I left, I wiped my tears away with holy water.

•

When I go to class later in the day, another boy I like looks at me and asks if I need a hug. We don't hug, and I'm happy, because touching him stings. I think about the nights he used to spend in my bed: his bare chest, the way it felt to have him pull my hair. Mostly, I think about how he told me that his dad passed away in high school, and how he's since spent time in rehab. How he's always sniffling because he used to do so much cocaine.

It makes me sort of sick how easy it is for me to love people. It also scares me that had I hugged him, I would've seen that as more intimate than the sex we used to have. It's like poet Ilya Kaminsky says: "You can fuck / anyone—but with whom can you sit in water?" A lot of the time, I dream about him and me sitting silently in a bathtub until our fingers prune. I wonder if he and his new girlfriend take showers together in the mornings.

Sometimes, I think God and sex are synonymous. The few times I've felt truly holy, like I was being taken care of by someone more powerful than you or I will ever be, I was doing something that some part of me said I shouldn't be. But a different, other part of me sighed and said, *Oh yes, this is exactly how it's supposed to be*.

After the first night I slept with this boy, a man on the street tried to hand me a Bible. I didn't take it, and I don't know if it was because I felt I already knew the way to heaven or because I felt unholy.

•

The rest of the week passes the way most of my weeks do. The world keeps spinning even though I'm afraid to live in this country and afraid of what the future holds come January. I go to my classes and do my homework. I go to the tattoo shop, sign all the forms, and chicken out right before the needle touches my skin. I get drunk on Thursday night and bring a boy home, but I don't let him touch me much and don't let him stay the night. On Friday, I go to a bar with the boy I like, and this time we do hug, and his hand sits on my lower back most of the night and I buy him soda after soda because he is sober and I am so proud of him. When I ask where his girlfriend is, he tells me she's across the street with friends. When I ask why he isn't with her, he shrugs and puts his hand on my waist. We dance.

On Sunday morning, I decide to go to church.

I choose a Unitarian church that speaks about tolerance and love and community on its website, and spend the entire morning beforehand wondering what to wear. I settle on black dress jeans, boat shoes, a red sweater. I wear my glasses and make sure my hair is combed. I don't know why I'm nervous; church is supposed to be the place where all are accepted and where anyone, no matter how broken, can be saved. I wonder if I'm afraid that I'll be viewed as broken and in need of saving, or if I actually am and do. I want to be welcomed, but I don't want it to happen out of pity.

When I arrive, nearly everyone else is in sweatpants or ripped jeans, some even still in their pajamas. One of the men working is wearing a University of Michigan jujitsu shirt and has a beard past his collarbones. It feels and looks more like a gymnasium inside than a church, only carpeted. A woman invites me to sit with her and her boyfriend and hands me a program. Before starting the service, a woman comes onstage and tells us that if we are unsure about our belief in God, then we should replace the word "God" with "love" whenever it's said. I resolve to go the "love" route. But then there is a live band, and though they sound nice, the songs are more traditional than I anticipated. The word "God" is mentioned so many times in the first minute, any hope I had of replacing it with the word "love" has gone out the window. I read the lyrics from the program and sing along hesitantly. I worry that everyone around me knows I'm new to the church and don't know what I'm doing. I worry my voice is the voice that can be heard painfully above everyone else's.

The band moves offstage and a woman with short brown hair, wearing a green sweater, replaces them. She holds a ball of tissues and warns us she will likely need them.

The church is silent, so many of us staring at our feet.

We wait patiently for her to compose herself. I am surprised that someone who identifies as Jewish would be at a Unitarian church rather than a synagogue, but the woman sitting next to me explains that the woman onstage is the cofounder of this church. When she can speak again, the cofounder gestures to her wife, who is sitting in the front row, and tells us about their identity as a Christian and Jewish couple. She tells us how fearful she is for every facet of this identity. Then she tells us we have to stick together, and that once we take care of ourselves and are mentally able to, we have to fight back against hatred and we'll have to keep fighting for four years. She says if Muslims have to go on a registry, we all have to register alongside them regardless of our religion, and the church erupts in cheers. I smile and cheer too. For a moment I feel a part of the group and not like an outsider. Does it matter whether I believe in God if I'm able to love alongside these people?

The cofounder sits down next to her wife, who places her arm around her shoulders. A man wearing a Black Lives Matter pin takes her place and begins his own sermon by speaking about how we have to stand tall at our Thanksgiving dinners two weeks from today. He makes a joke about how hard politics can be to navigate, and says that next week's service will focus on how to handle Thanksgiving. I think of my own father and the majority of my extended family and their conservative Republican values, and feel comforted by the idea that this church could help guide my time at home in some way.

He quickly shifts gears by reading a passage out of the Bible, and I immediately feel suffocated by the formality of his words. The passage is about Jesus telling his followers that they'll be persecuted for believing in him, but that they must not fight against the persecution because God will give them the words to say when they are questioned, and the actions to perform when they're called upon by him. My discomfort increases as he continues to preach. He ends the sermon by inviting the band back to the stage, where they sing a song together, and I once again sing along, reading the lines off my program. People in the audience begin to raise their hands and look to the sky, smiling. I know they are having an intimate moment with God. In their minds, it's just them and him in this room. I take Communion, something I haven't done since I was eight, as the band sings and they continue to raise their hands, and I feel small.

•

That night, I sit in my bed and think about God and who I can invite over. I think it's desperate of me to want to booty-call some-one at eight on a Sunday night, but I want to forget. I don't necessarily know what I'm looking to forget, but I know there is something inside me that needs to disappear, at least for the moment. It's probably that I'm lonely. To be honest, I likely need a therapist a lot more than I need religion.

When I was fourteen, I climbed to the top of a church at three in the morning after I'd just seen a movie. It was August, and though it had been hot during the day, my teeth were chattering now that the sun had gone down. The boy I was with was cold as well, so he put his arm around me and I laid my head on his chest and snuggled into him. We blamed it on need-ing warmth, but I think we wanted to be close to each other. It took time for our eyes to adjust to the darkness, but once they did, the sky was beaming with stars. I pointed out Orion; he showed me the Big Dipper. After a while, I saw my first shooting star. In that moment, I felt I didn't need to wish for anything. I felt like the rhythm of his heartbeat and the way the earth turned and my own breath were all in harmony.

I wasn't looking for God then, but I felt how I think people feel when they believe in him. I've felt it other times:

The New Year's Eve when I was drinking in the back of a car speeding down Lake Shore Drive and watching fireworks explode over the lake while M83 played and all the windows were rolled down.

The day I woke up surrounded by friends on a sailboat in the Caribbean to a double rainbow stretching over an island in the distance.

The day I took acid in the Chicago Botanic Garden with a boy I was just beginning to fall in love with and laughed until my stomach hurt and everything felt so beautiful I thought I would burst.

I felt it when I lost my virginity on a snowy winter night in Chicago to someone who would become my first love.

It sometimes feels like most of life is just suffering and begging: to be understood, or for someone to listen, or to be held. I think I beg more than others.
Maybe there's no sense in begging if you know that there will be moments of
being understood and being listened to and being held along the way. There
will be rooftops and boys and sex and people who pick up the phone even
after eight months of silence. I think that maybe I'm thinking about God all
wrong; that maybe God is just love and I've already found him. And in that
case, if Bright Eyes says that love's an excuse to hurt, then I'm a wound and a
knife all in one and I'm begging for us to hurt together.

I Googled "Borderline Personality Disorder" and Wanted to Run for the Hills

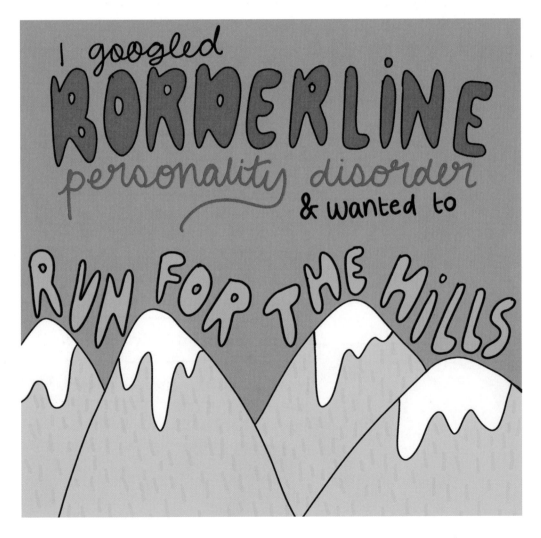

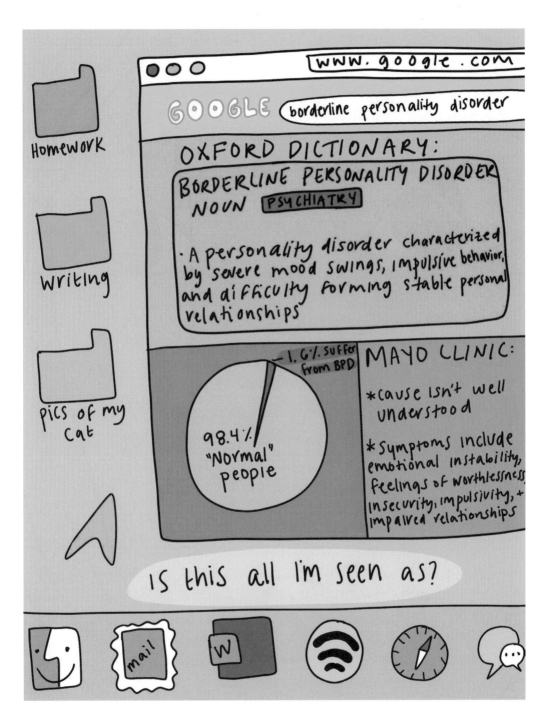

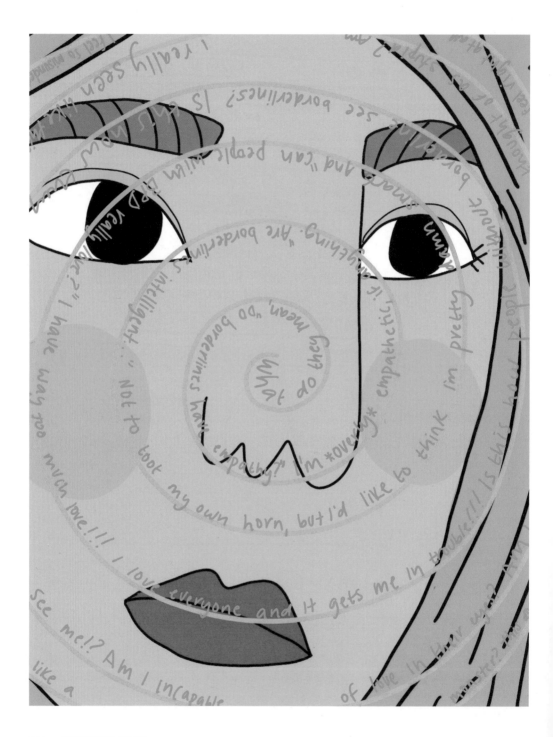

why do these sound so scary?

www.google.com

BPD IN POP CULTURE/MEDIA

NOTES

REMINDER: FEED THE CAT	TV/MOVIES
	· crazy ex-Girlfriend
DOCTORS APPT Jan 7	· maniac
	· Fatal Attraction
Buy milk	· Girl, Interrupted *
	* also a book
Poem due Jan 13	
	BOOKS
	· I hate you-don't leave me
	· sometimes I act crazy

why isn't there more out there?

PEOPLE ALSO ASK...
Are people with BPD dangerous?
Are borderlines abusive?
Are borderlines sociopaths?
Can people with BPD live normally?
What celebrity has BPD?
CLICK!
jeffrey dahmer
-diagnosed with BPD
-convicted of seventeen murders of men + boys
-necrophiliac
-cannibal
that's wildly discouraging...

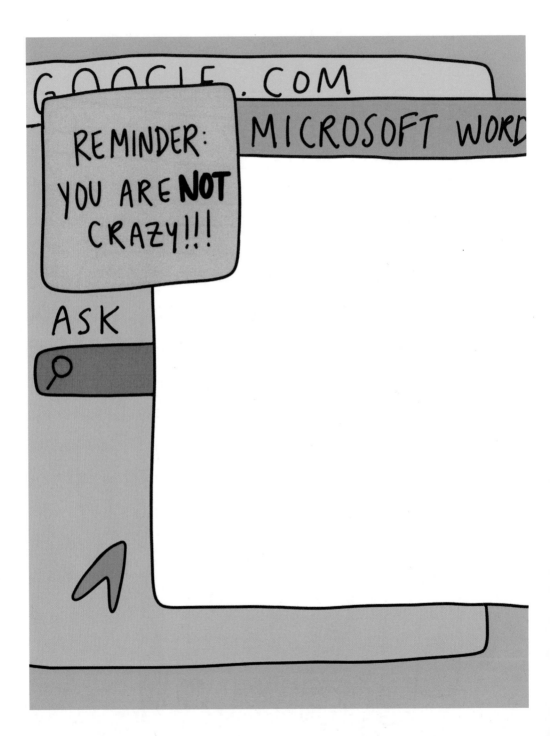

I'd Die for Mini Corndogs and Various Other Obsessions

1. I've fallen in love with a lot of things in my life:

2. When I love something, I love hard and fully, a Romeo and Juliet, I'll-kill-myself-to-be-with-you type of love.

3. But to call it "love" might be a misnomer. I did not love the barista; I wanted to become her and emulated her every action. I did not love the color pink; I transformed my bedroom and wardrobe into a sort of monochromatic haven where any other color was outlawed. I do not love–I become. I embody. I obsess.

4. According to *Merriam-Webster*:

Obsession: a persistent disturbing preoccupation with an often-unreasonable idea or feeling

Love: 1) strong affection for another arising out of kinship or personal ties, 2) warm attachment, enthusiasm, or devotion, or 3) the object of attachment, devotion, or admiration

5. I find it hard to see the difference between these two words.

6. Where do these obsessions (loves???) come from?

Mini corndogs:

- When I was young, I only played with miniature toys
    - I called them "little things"
    - I'd play for hours
    - I liked that you had to take great care to play with something so small

- I used to eat mini corndogs at a diner beneath my therapist's office before my sessions
    - Before I went to treatment, the last meal I had in the "real world" was mini corndogs
        - I think they made me feel safe

Pink:

- I was opposed to liking pink for a long time because I liked to be a contrarian
    - But then one day I thought, *This is too much work*
    - I decided it was okay to like "girly" things
- A girl I never met but who went to my college Instagrammed herself in all pink and I thought she looked cool
    - She seemed to have a lot of friends who loved her
    - I wanted to be her
        - Or have her life
    - She seemed happy
        - I wanted to be happy

7. It seems that the root of my obsessions is the idea that if I had, or did, or became, this one thing or person, I would feel content, satisfied, whole.

8. The problem with this line of thinking is that no matter what I acquire, I'm still the one who acquired it. No matter whom I emulate, I am still, ultimately, me.

9. What does it mean to be me?

10. **I know I like:** writing, art, sunflowers, reading, smoking weed, drawing, designing greeting cards, eating chocolate-covered bananas, listening to music, wearing mom jeans.

I know I dislike: itchy things, most seafood, conservative politics, when my dog shits in the house, depression, anxiety, closing my eyes in the shower, scary stories told in the light or dark.

11. Is that all there is to a person? Their likes and dislikes?

12. Let's try this again.

13. **I feel:** frustrated that I've lived twenty-four years and don't have the hang of who I am more.

     I wonder: Is happiness a constant state of being, or something more fleeting? Is feeling consistently happy possible, or is that an idealized goal?

     I am afraid: that I can trace everything that I know about myself back to people I've been obsessed with in the past.

14. In the borderline community, a person you are obsessed with is called your "favorite person," or FP. An FP is more than a best friend, or a lover. An FP is more akin to an idol, someone who can do no wrong. By projecting your beliefs and ideals onto your FP, they become exactly what you need that person to be. In this way, the FP is perfect.

15. Various FPs I've had throughout my life, in no particular order:

My best friend in the fourth grade:
- Always wanted to solve a Rubik's cube
- Was allowed to paint on her walls
- Drew monsters a lot
- Wore tutus to school

My BFF freshman year of college:
- Illustrator
- Thought relationships that didn't end in marriage were failures
- Now a famous model
- Once Instagrammed herself eating ice cream while pooping

Fourth grade BFF's sister:
- Artist who painted a series of murderers
- Had a taxidermy collection
- Was dating a bisexual guy who always wore a mustard-colored tweed suit (whom I had a crush on)
- Left her vibrator out in the open

16. To simply be around or be friends with my FP is not enough. I want to swallow the person whole, become a clone, be so alike people cannot tell us apart from each other. I shed my old personality like snakeskin and try the other person on. It feels good to be someone who isn't me, to get out of this mind and body for a bit. I begin to dress like the FP. I mimic the person's laugh. I dive into the person's interests. I cannot stop talking about the FP to anyone who will listen. I, for a moment, am not Courtney, a girl who knows only a handful of things about herself. I am the FP, but also me, a sort of conjoined twin. For once, I feel like I know who I am. The unstable sense of self and emptiness that accompany borderline fade away.

17. To have an FP is part of a common borderline pattern called idealization and devaluation.

18.

Idealization: the practice of putting someone on a pedestal: of idolizing, obsessing over, and viewing the person as perfect

Devaluation: the practice of regarding something or someone as worthless or completely flawed

19. Because an FP is an idealized version of an individual, the idea that the person is perfect can never be sustained. Eventually, the facade I've created for the FP will break down, revealing a real human, complete with flaws and defects like the rest of us.

20. When the illusion is shattered, I fall into devaluation. I curse the time I spent with the FP, feeling abandoned by a persona that never truly existed, and horrified that this person will not cure me of my loneliness, emptiness, or sadness.

21. Losing an FP causes me to collapse in on myself. It doesn't matter what else I have going on in my life—I feel like I have nothing left to live for.

22. What now?

23. Until I can find another FP, I go back to relying on obsessions that cannot leave me, that remain perfect, that do not have a facade.

24. I eat mini corndogs, hoping they'll heal me from the inside.

A by-no-means comprehensive LIST of things that have Scared me half to death

1. The Green Ribbon, which I listened to on an *IN a Dark, Dark Room* tape at a friend's house in third grade. When they described removing the ribbon and the girl's head falling off, I lost my shit and tried to pretend my sobbing was caused by an allergy attack. We never hung out again.

2. My friend Emily told me the song "Last Christmas" by wham! was about a dad literally giving his daughter his heart and subsequently dying. "Allergy" attack!!!!

3. My parent's dog, Jersey, who usually ignores me, began to follow me around and sleep in my bed and I convinced myself I had a horrific illness I didn't know about that he could somehow smell, and that he was only being affectionate because he knew I was dying.

4. I ordered spicy peanut noodles and believed I was going to discover I'd recently grown allergic to peanuts and die on the spot, which oddly didn't stop me from eating them.

Dear   , I'm Sorry I Exist

Dear   ,
~~I'm sorry~~

Dear   ,
I'm sorry I

ugh

Dear   ,
I'm sorry I took that Polaroid of you while you were sleeping.

Dear   ,
I'm sorry I thought you talking to someone else at a party meant you were abandoning me so I convinced all our friends to hate you.

Dear   ,
I'm sorry I told you that I knew you thought I was a charity case and that you were friends with me only to be nice, even though I had no proof of this at all.

Dear   ,
I'm sorry I was acting weird at the Van Gogh Museum in Amsterdam and I told you I had jet lag when really I was still rolling on liquid Molly I took the night before.

Dear   ,
I'm sorry I microwaved a cookie for fifteen minutes to see what would happen and caused the school microwave to explode and everyone to get assigned seats at lunch because I refused to come forward and say that I was the one who made the microwave explode because I wanted to know what would happen if I microwaved a tiny butter cookie for fifteen minutes.

Dear   ,

I'm sorry for the night I spent staring at that bobblehead of you that you said was from a bar mitzvah (but how could it have been from a bar mitzvah when it had a full beard?), which nodded yes at us the entire time even though inside my head I was like *no no no no no no.*

Dear   ,

I'm sorry you took me on vacation to Laguna Beach and I sat in the hotel room the whole time feeling sick to my stomach because my boyfriend had fallen off his bike and gotten stitches.

Dear   ,
I'm sorry I convinced myself you were a bad friend who spoke to me only when you wanted something from me, even though I'd actually abandoned you for the ~luv of my lyfe~

Dear   ,
I'm sorry I told you that you looked like Bob Saget when you got a weird haircut.

Dear   ,
I'm sorry to be this person, but I really do think acid cured my depression for six months.

Dear   ,
I'm sorry I made a huge scene about us not hanging out all summer and accused you of thinking I was just a "school friend" even though you'd written me a love note in which you called me your drug.

Dear   ,
I'm sorry I told everyone the love note you wrote me was weird even though I still have it saved seven years later.

Dear   ,
I'm sorry I told you I thought I'd done crack when I think I actually just had a panic attack from weird weed.

Dear   ,
I'm sorry I told everyone you proposed to me and left out the detail that we were thirteen and it was in the milk aisle of a mini-mart.

Dear   ,
I'm sorry I went on vacation, suddenly started to hate you, and then broke up with you over the phone after a year of dating while you cried in your best friend's closet.

Dear   ,
I'm sorry I begged you to take me back three days later.

Dear   ,
I'm sorry I was so giddy after we spent the day together that I got up at 5:00 a.m. and bought everyone donuts.

Dear   ,
I'm sorry I blamed not being attracted to you anymore on my depression.

Dear   ,
I'm sorry I met you once and then told everyone I saw that you were my "future husband."

Dear   ,
I'm sorry I interpreted seeing my first shooting star while we were cuddling as proof we were fated to be together.

Dear   ,
I'm sorry I told you I was going to marry you and then broke up with you less than a year later.

Dear   ,
I'm sorry I exist.

Dear   ,

I'm sorry I took your lack of response when I asked if we were exclusive as a yes, and then got mad at you for sleeping with someone else.

Dear   ,

I'm sorry I cried in your bedroom for three hours–thinking about the time you played me John Mayer on your guitar–while all your housemates listened to me sob because your bedroom was right off the living area.

Dear   ,

I'm sorry I made you stay with me in a hotel room in the Tenderloin after that time I wailed in your room while all your housemates listened.

Dear   ,

I'm sorry I obsessed over you for six months even though we only had sex three times.

Dear   ,

I'm sorry I wrote your Georgetown Law essay even though I was in the hospital having my airway monitored, and I'm also sorry you got in.

Dear   ,

I'm sorry I used Alan Rickman dying as an excuse to cheat on you.

Dear   ,

I'm sorry I worried you.

Dear   ,
I'm sorry I called you every day from the psych ward even though I knew it was pushing you further away.

Dear   ,
I'm sorry I kept threatening to jump off the tenth-story balcony at your bar mitzvah.

Dear   ,
I'm sorry I told you I jumped off my roof when what I actually did was think about jumping off my roof but was too afraid of heights to go through with it.

Dear   ,
I'm sorry I didn't get angry that time you asked me if I was a cutter and then questioned me about why I didn't have more scars when I said yes.

Dear   ,
I'm sorry I couldn't help you dissect that fetal pig in biology class and instead got myself hospitalized in a psych ward because the pig freaked me out so bad that I wanted to be as dead as the pig.

Dear   ,
I'm sorry for

Dear   ,
I'm sorry I

Dear   ,
I'm sorry

Dear
Dear
Dear

I'm sorry

Oops, I'm Bleeding Again

He turns on the lights, and as if by instinct, my hand reaches toward the lamp and the room is dark again. He turns them on, and again, the instinct. Darkness.

I am an easy crier: tampon commercials, abandoned gloves left in the snow, a dog tied up outside CVS the entire time I eat at the café across the street. It's been two months of togetherness and he has not seen it yet; he thinks I've exaggerated my tendency to bawl over the little things.

For the most part, I can control my body. I wait until he's in another room to fart. I don't poop until I'm home, alone. I stifle burps. Cough to mask the sound of my stomach's gurgling.

But this? This I can't control. Tears stream down my temples, fall into the wells of my ears.

"I love your body," he says, wiping away the salt. I turn to face the window, my back toward him.

I've gained forty-five pounds since starting Abilify. But this is not why I'm crying.

I accept the softness of my stomach, the rash that ignites on warm days at the insides of my thighs when they rub together as I walk. I accept that I cannot button some of the pants I've worn comfortably for years, that my BMI lists me as overweight. What matters is that I am alive to see these things when, for so long, I didn't want to be. I am okay with this trade-off: the side effect of insatiable hunger in exchange for a medicine that keeps me from wanting to die.

My softness is not why I'm crying.

"Talk to me," George says.

I stare out the window, watch a man and his dog pass by. How can I even explain?

"Let's just keep the lights off, okay?" I say, trying not to sound like I'm begging. "We can leave them on in two weeks."

"What's the difference between two weeks and now?" he asks.

I kiss him and stick my hand down his pants. He relaxes, lets out a small sigh, kisses me back in the darkness. "Just give me time," I say into his mouth. What I leave out: *to heal.*

•

When I stand in front of the mirror, I get tunnel vision. I do not care about flyaway hairs, the new pimple pushing its way to the surface of my chin, the purple-tinted stretch marks I recently discovered streaking the bottoms of my breasts. I do not see my cheeks turning red, but I feel the heat of their flush. And though I am ashamed, and I want nothing more than for the real issue–the one thing that does actually bother me when I look at my body–to leave my life permanently, I can't help myself. Automatically, my eyes and fingers find their way to my pubic hair, to the scabs that litter the area, and I pick myself open.

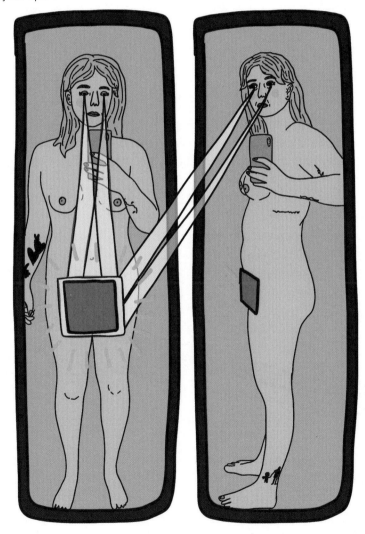

The relief is instant, palpable. I sigh, partly because I'm frustrated I've restarted the healing process yet again, partly because this is my high. I've experimented with coke, Molly, shrooms, acid, drunk an entire fifth of vodka in a night; nothing touches this feeling. The excitement as my nail first lifts the scab, the subtle, sometimes sharp pain as it's peeled from my body, the spreading calm as blood pools in what's left behind. I find my breath. My shoulders fall. I close my eyes, trace my fingers along my skin until I settle on the next scab. I pick.

I pick.

I pick.

•

My pubes are a war zone, marked by scars and gaping holes and scabs barely holding back blood and, often, yellow-green pus. When I go to the bathroom, I sit on the toilet and stare at my horror. My stomach churns as I look at what I've damaged, where I can open myself next. If I'm in the good light of my bathroom at home, I take note of what I believe needs fixing, then head to the cabinet, retrieve tweezers, and begin to dig. Either there, standing by the light of the window, or, if I can bear to wait the seven steps it takes me to get back to my room, in the comfort of my bed. If I am not home, my bitten-down nails suffice as my tool. I rarely leave a bathroom without bleeding, or the intention of doing so later.

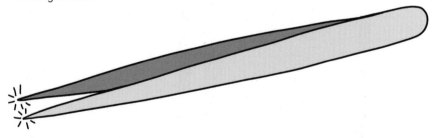

I use my free hand to pull my pubic hair to the side to expose the razor-burn bumps underneath, the ingrown hairs begging to be released, the hairs I justify plucking by convincing myself they're ingrown, the hairs I swear I can see beneath the skin but dig and dig and dig and find no trace of. With pointed tweezers, I work. I scrape away at the skin until a hair appears, like buried treasure. I sit and focus and pluck and excavate until that hair is free. If my tweezers cannot grasp the hair, I feel my pulse rise. I hold my breath. Anger boils in my stomach. My chest constricts. My hands shake, making it even harder to retrieve the hair. My frustration grows.

Until the release. Then, the feeling of complete and utter bliss, better than the first bite of Lucky Charms or a toe-curling orgasm or being asked on a date by a ten. All the tension that had built up over not being able to remove the hair melts away in a glorious, warm flood that radiates through my entire body, starting from the newly bald patch where once was pubic hair, now replaced with open skin and blood. And the tension that came from not being able to remove the hair, the stress of the day, all anxiety, any fear–gone. Just like that.

•

I remember sitting in Native American literature class my junior year of high school, googling therapists that specialized in obsessive-compulsive disorder, or OCD. My body was covered in Band-Aids; mostly my upper arms, the crack of my ass, my pubes. When I was anxious, I picked, and I was anxious all the time. Prom and spring break were on the horizon, and I wanted to be clear, clean. I e-mailed my mom and therapist, telling them that I needed help, that my lifelong picking habit was, maybe, just a little bit, slightly, out of control. I was sick of the white and purple scars the scabs left behind, the ugliness of the scabs at all. I wanted to undress in front of my then-boyfriend without hiding beneath a blanket, wanted not to feel the need to cover scabs with makeup, and most of all, wanted to feel in control again. Because although picking gave me control over my body and anxieties when I began, somewhere along the way, I'd become powerless to its urge.

•

When I began to see the OCD specialist, I was hopeful. The first step in fixing a problem is admitting you have a problem in the first place, and that's often said to be the hardest part. I thought that because I'd made the effort to start therapy, the struggle was nearly over. Instead, I was just beginning to understand my diagnosis. The therapist informed me that though I had OCD tendencies, my actions didn't take up a large enough part of my day to be considered full-blown OCD. Instead, he said, I was suffering from dermatillomania and trichotillomania. Compulsive skin picking and hair pulling.

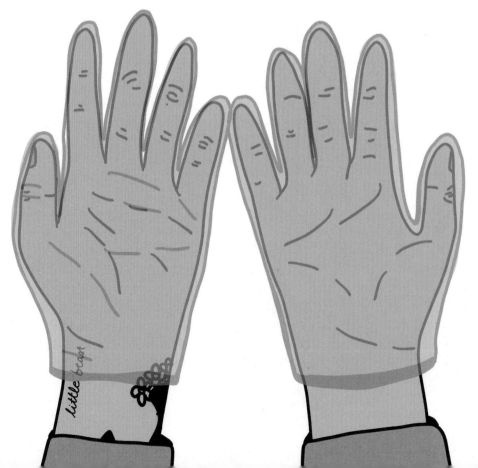

When I was first hospitalized for my depression in the seventh grade, I met a kind girl named Anne. Anne began the program with a bald spot on the crown of her head as if she were an old man, and within a week, her head was completely bare. She said she hadn't realized she was doing it, that her hands just found their way to her scalp and pulled. It didn't hurt like you'd think it would. "It felt good until I looked in the mirror," she said.

I thought of Anne when I was diagnosed, and every time I slipped my fingers into the vinyl gloves the specialist required me to wear at home, which my mom duct-taped onto my hands so I couldn't pull them off myself. I slept in the gloves. I ate with the gloves on. My hands sweated inside the gloves. Did homework with the gloves, held a pencil through the gloves. But I couldn't wear them all the time; I had to go to school, exist in public. People wouldn't understand. And, predictably, each time the duct tape was peeled from my skin and my clammy hands were released from their vinyl prison, I picked.

I stopped seeing the doctor.

•

Most of the time, before, there is bargaining: *You can choose one scab to pick* and *Only picking, no digging* and *Only where your underwear hides*. Always, justification: *That hair is ingrown anyways* and *That scab is basically ready to fall off* and *It's been a long day, you deserve some relief*. Inevitably, I break my own rules. Plucking one hair becomes two becomes eight. The promise to dig at an ingrown hair only "a little" becomes gouging at my skin until the area stops bleeding, so deep the wound won't close for days. Sometimes, I question whether I'm looking for a hair at all, or whether what I saw and so desperately feel the need to remove is a vein.

I try to stop myself: before vacations, when I'll be seen in a swimsuit, when I know I'm going to get laid. I buy Neosporin and Band-Aids and cover my body in them. I clench my fists when I want to pick, throw away my tweezers, try and bite my nails instead. I think of my shame, what it would be like to be naked without makeup on my pussy, what it would mean to be clear for the first time in years. To let even my scars fade. To be normal.

Sometimes, I go days. On some of my best tries, a week. If I'm especially stubborn, maybe a week and a half. Sometimes, I'm able to look in the mirror and think, *If I keep this up, I won't need the concealer anymore.* Sometimes, *This time is really it.* But always, life happens, and I'm right back where I started, bleeding beneath my pants, the relief picking brings me settling into frustration and horror.

•

Before our third date, George texted me a picture of a graphic narrative I've published, one that's about living with borderline personality disorder. He commented on the style of the drawings and said he liked the story. I panicked, made an emergency appointment with my therapist, and talked to her on the phone as I picked and picked and picked to comfort myself. This is the scariest part of dating for me: When do I reveal my diagnosis? Is not revealing my disorder a type of lie? Would he leave me once he knew the ways I suffer? I text back something about color choices and line weight, trying to keep the conversation on the techniques I'd used rather than content. He didn't push.

We talked about my disorder on our date that Friday. I was too scared to say my diagnosis out loud. In the In-N-Out drive-through he yelled:

I told him I was surprised I wasn't crying. He said I had nothing to be ashamed of. This made me want to cry more.

I went through my history in a fast, brief way: the hospitalizations, the struggle for diagnosis, the way that borderline's symptoms manifested as cutting and not eating when I was young. I assured him I'm better, or as "better" as I can be. I'm on good medications, I eat when I'm hungry, I haven't cut since I was fifteen. I framed it carefully: *I haven't cut since I was fifteen.* I did not say: *I don't self-harm.*

That night, we fucked for the first time. I kept the lights off. He felt close to me, thought we'd broken down a wall between us. I am always afraid to share that I have borderline; I wonder if I ever won't be. But when I was diagnosed, I made a promise to myself and the BPD community that I'd try to diminish some of the stigma surrounding my, our, diagnosis. When I began publishing writing and art about suffering from borderline, I knew what I was getting

myself into. That in order to be an advocate, I'd have to be vulnerable. That moment with George was inevitable, and though I am never fully comfortable with revealing my diagnosis, I was, in some ways, prepared.

In the morning, I dressed facing away from him. He thought it was because we were newly coupled, that the level where we could be comfortably naked around each other had not yet been reached. When I pulled on my underwear, I looked at my cuts and thanked God I had never written about them.

•

I try to stop picking so George and I can fuck with the lights on—I really do. I go through the whole routine: wearing oven mitts when I'm home, not allowing myself to glance down when I'm on the toilet so I won't have the urge, biting my nails short so I don't have the ability to pick without tweezers, hiding my tweezers, making the pilgrimage to CVS for Neosporin and Band-Aids. For a few days, I heal. I'm optimistic. I'm in remission. Cured.

I get to the point where I need to cover only my scars, not new cuts, with makeup, and I'm proud. *Soon, I'll be okay*, I think. In a week I'll allow him to see me in all my naked, healed glory, and he won't know anything was ever wrong.

•

"Let's take a shower," George says.

My two weeks are up, and, like I always do, I've failed. A week and a half of healing was eradicated in one night of getting high and sitting with a flashlight pointed at my pubes, a pair of tweezers ruining everything I'd worked so hard to fix. It's always worse after I try to stop. What would usually be five cuts is fifteen. They're swollen and red and disgusting and I want to stop existing in my body, to not have a body at all, to be, just this once, fucking normal and to let myself have pubes or no pubes or some pubes and not care, like the rest of the world.

"With the lights off?" I ask. He answers with his eyes and furrowed, strong eyebrows, and I begin to cry.

We sit cross-legged on the bed, facing each other. When I try to look away, he guides my chin back to face him. We're only two months into this thing, so new to labels and "I love you"s. I worry I'm too much, that my borderline is already a burden, that the weight of my past self-harm behaviors will break us under the admission that I never actually stopped, that I simply found a new way to hurt myself. Better places, better ways of hiding.

I take a deep breath.

In typical borderline fashion, every time I've met a new partner, I've been quick to fall in love, quick to tell family and friends that, no, I'm being serious, this time it's different. And every time, it's the same. But when I met George, something in my body sighed a sigh that said, *This time, it's real*. I trust him. I think of the way he reacted when he found out about my diagnosis, how I begged him not to say the words "borderline personality disorder" out loud and the way he screamed them anyway, proving that there was nothing to be ashamed of. At least not in front of him.

His expression is soft, and I feel as if I'm letting him down whether I gather the courage to tell him or continue keeping my secret. No matter what, I suffer from trichotillomania and dermatillomania. No matter what, the cuts beneath my underwear will scream loud red against my pale skin.

I explain: the powerful urge to pick and pull, the tension that builds when I'm doing so, the overwhelming release once it's over. The cyclicality of it. That I've tried to get help. That I can't stop. That I wish I were normal. That I understand if he doesn't want to fuck me–be with me–now that he knows. That everyone in my life believes I've been clean from self-harm for nine years and yet I make myself bleed daily. I used to cut my wrists and thighs with the sharp ends of tweezers. Now I just use them in a different way. Either way, I'm bleeding.

"That's it?" George asks when I'm finished. "That you pick at your pubes?"

"You don't get it," I say. "It's awful and unsightly and disgusting and I hate that I do it."

"Courtney, we all have issues," he says. "Let's make a plan so you can stop."

"I get if you don't want to fuck me anymore," I say.

"You could do anything down there and I'd want to fuck you," he says, and we laugh.

For a moment, I allow myself to be hopeful. I do not think of every time I've tried to stop, of all the times I've failed, of the OCD doctor who didn't help, the duct-taped-on gloves, the fact that I'm too afraid to share my problem with even my therapist. I do not think of the cuts beneath my pubes or the bald patches surrounding them. I take his hand and we walk to the bathroom, where I undress while staring at the light switch that I do not touch. He looks me in the eyes, and then moves his eyes down my body, stopping at the meeting of my thighs.

"Okay," he says.

"Okay," I say back, turning the shower on, lights blaring.

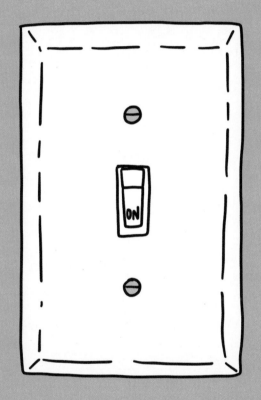

How caring for ailing senior pets helps me care for myself

1. I like to care for animals who perhaps aren't most people's first choice; someone overlooked, maybe a little hard to love, someone who has seen some shit. I have also seen some shit, and to give them a good life now is my way of healing, controlling, their (and my) past.

2. When I got my first dog, Pinot, he shared his previous name with a boy I'd been deeply, scarily obsessed with. Each time I cared for Pinot, I felt I was wiping the slate clean; he was someone I was not "crazy" with—I was caring, and gentle, and kind.

3. Pinot had a whole host of medical issues, and was diagnosed right as I was with borderline. Caring for Pinot helped me show compassion toward myself; giving him medicated baths helped me remember to put Neosporin on the cuts I gave myself from digging out my pubic hair, giving him his medication helped me feel comfortable enough to take my own, taking him for walks got me out of bed on days I wanted to stay in it forever.

4. No matter how annoying or frustrating it was to have a dog as anxious and ridden with separation anxiety as Francie, my second dog, she made me feel wanted and loved in a way anyone would be lucky to feel.

Ode to the Psychiatrist I Hate Who Gives Me Good Drugs

I like for the therapists I see to be a sort of version of myself, like a more put-together me whom I can project my thoughts and feelings and general life onto. A me who isn't me. A me ten years in the future, able to help people instead of needing to be helped. As a result, I've pretty much exclusively seen blond, blue-eyed therapists who are around five foot three. I want to talk to a wiser, more mature version of myself. Therapy acts as a type of mirror pep talk, only more productive because my reflection talks back.

I am superficial when it comes to therapists. If you don't look cool, I won't let you in. I once met a therapist who wore clogs, and the second I saw her, I knew I wasn't going to tell her anything substantial about my life. I am not a clog wearer, and I don't feel that a clog wearer would understand me. This is a pretty nonsensical assumption, but I go with my gut. The only time clogs are acceptable is if you're a psychic, because psychics transcend all laws of fashion and general aspects of being. A psychic could show up naked and I'd probably be even more inclined to believe what she was saying. With psychics, it's the weirder, the better.

cool clogs

I currently have a brunette therapist, which might seem to be outside my norm, but I am okay with her hair color because she reminds me of Shoshanna from HBO's TV show *Girls*. Shoshanna went blond for a few seasons, so she's essentially on the periphery of looking like me, and besides, I've always found Shoshanna hilarious, and have been compared to her character in the past. She would never wear clogs unless ironically. Or maybe the cool clogs that you see at Urban Outfitters, the ones that only super-chic people can pull off and make look good. So, my current therapist, once again, reminds me of myself.

uncool clogs

When I go to therapy and see her, I feel like I am a comedian. She laughs at everything I say, so sometimes I spend half the time we have together just trying to make her laugh. I consistently go to therapy because it is what I have to do to keep myself alive, but when my life is going well, it feels like a chore. I have to fill time, make things funny, avoid feeling like I have nothing worthwhile to share. Life is pretty boring at the moment, and by boring, I mean nothing is going wrong. I am so used to living in extremes that now that I've found medications that keep me stable, things feel almost monotonous. I am wrapping up the final year of my MFA program, this book is set to be published, I have a new boyfriend that I love and a job lined up after graduation, yet I'm saying life is boring. It's silly. I'm grateful to be bored, though, because it means things are going well. If I'm trying to fill time in therapy, life must be good.

And it is, albeit quiet. I am on a first-name basis with some of the cashiers at Trader Joe's. I spend most of my time alone with my dog, Francie, asking her questions she can't respond to. Most days, we go on a walk, but some days we nap through walk time. I eat a lot of frozen meals, such as diet macaroni from Trader Joe's. I write, or try to. I get high in my bed and blow smoke out the window, hoping that my roommates don't realize I'm smoking in the house. I usually call my mom two or three times over the course of a day just to check in or fill time. On Mondays, Wednesdays, and Fridays, I go to class. After class on Wednesdays every other week, I go to therapy. And once a month, I see my psychiatrist.

My psychiatrist is rotund in a jolly, Mrs. Claus type of way, and has action figures all over her office. I once re-marked that the room smelled like sunscreen, and she told me she'd gotten a new air freshener, and I felt bad for the rest of the day. She definitely goes to Renaissance fairs in her free time, and is into anime, if the figurines around her office are any indication of her personal life. I'm not knocking these things, I'm just saying they're not

for me. She falls out of my typical category of doctor, because I am unable to project myself onto her. But I keep seeing her because she's covered by my insurance, and because the one time I tried to go off my medication I became instantly suicidal and was hospitalized for over a week. Most importantly, I see her because she keeps my life boring.

I should clarify: it's Lexapro, Abilify, and Vyvanse that keep my life boring, but she is my dealer, and I'm bound to her because of it.

Before I began taking medication, my life was exciting, and simultaneously unlivable. My emotions flew up and down over the course of a day, ranging from suicidal to euphoric, usually triggered by small things. One day I woke up feeling on top of the world, until I dropped the Eggo waffle I'd just microwaved and, suddenly, life wasn't worth living. I scream-cried to my mom that I wanted to die, crumpled in a pile on the floor.

She kept me home from school to monitor me, making sure I didn't do anything drastic over a freezer-burned breakfast item. It wasn't really the waffle–it couldn't have been–but there was something inside me that was always looking for a reason to explode. Everything was a wild ride. ASPCA commercial? Sure to make me want to off myself. A first kiss? Undoubtedly my future life partner and thus deserving of obsession. Didn't receive a text back? Worthy of slicing my arms up over.

waffle worth my ending my life over

doesn't even have butter or maple syrup

Borderline personality disorder

major depression

me

Anxiety

Before medication, the mundane was riveting because everything was a mystery to me. I never knew how I'd react to situations, so I lived life on the edge of my seat, unable to anticipate what was coming next. Most of my reactions were bad and resulted in some form of self-harm, but when things were good, they were magical. That's the only way I know how to describe it. When things were good, I felt the world was made for me, like I was living in a utopia or a very good version of *The Truman Show*, like everything came together for this moment, for me, here, now. It was like being on acid without the hallucinogenic aspects, just a feeling of magical synchronicity with the universe. Every person I kissed was my soul mate, every A I received was because I was a genius, every friend I made was the friendship that would put all others to shame. But when things were bad, everything acted as proof that I was an unlovable, hated, monstrous person undeserving of space on the planet. I often cycled through these emotions more than once a day, like a roller coaster ride I didn't pay to get on. At times it was fun, but mostly it was exhausting.

I think of myself as the intersection of a three-part Venn diagram, whose elements are borderline personality disorder, major depression, and anxiety, with me stuck in the middle. All these elements come together to make me the level of kooky that I am, or what many would call "crazy." I could reclaim that title, but I don't feel the desire to. I want to be normal. I want to be boring.

At any given time, the three parts compete against one another. My borderline brain tells me to categorize everything because, to it, there is no such thing as a space between good and bad. People are friends or enemies; I am either loved or wished dead; everything is right, or everything is wrong. It then wants me to act on these beliefs, a course that leads to disaster, always. I have never acted on a borderline thought that didn't end up getting me in trouble.

Borderline competes with my depression, because it calls for action, whereas depression sucks the life out of me. My depressed brain is one of lifelessness, like an unbearable void that I have no desire to unearth myself from. There is No Point to anything, so why list things, people, places at all? Who cares if they are good or evil?

But my borderline brain cares. My anxious brain believes the world is ending and there are signs everywhere: the radio cutting out, my dog looking strangely into space, the lights taking a moment to flicker on. And if the world isn't ending, *my* world is. Every stomach gurgle is a sign of my imminent death, my racing heartbeat and dry throat just a confirmation of my demise.

As these three parts compete inside me, I have to fight back somehow. And though I've tried meditating, seeing a life coach, getting acupuncture, doing yoga, and changing my diet, the only thing that has ever helped is medication. My medication is my first line of defense, taking the edge off my irrational thoughts, telling everything necessary to fuck right off. It calms me down and allows me to take a step back and survey what I'd otherwise be directly thrust into. It doesn't clear the storm, but it gives me enough insight to see where it's headed next, and what's the best way to prepare for any destruction it causes.

It took me years to find the right medication cocktail of Lexapro, Vyvanse, and Abilify to keep me afloat. I struggled through crippling side effects like weight gain, brain fog, migraines, and an irregular heartbeat, which led me straight to the emergency room. I have full years of my life that feel like a blur of overmedication on a drug that I was told to take four times a day, which only made my anxiety worse. I once took a medication intended to help me that made me want to off myself right then and there—something I thought existed only in the warnings at the end of medication commercials on TV. Even now, I suffer from vivid, and often horrifying, dreams, and a feeling of sluggishness as a side effect of my Lexapro, which I try to level out by taking a higher dose of Vyvanse. My Abilify has made me gain forty-five pounds, which is doing a number on my self-esteem, counteracting its purpose of making me happier. It isn't a perfect science, but I'd rather not fit into my pants and be tired than want to die.

My psychiatrist does her best. When I tell her I am gaining weight, or exhausted all the time, she offers me solutions. We up my Vyvanse to counteract the unending hunger I feel from my Abilify and the brain fog from my Lexapro. She gives me beta-blockers for when Vyvanse makes me feel overstimulated, like I'm crawling out of my skin. She prescribes Ativan for when I have panic attacks that nothing else can begin to touch. She gives me advice; tells me to work out, track my calories, set up a routine, drink more caffeine. Our conversations are fifteen minutes at most and filled with awkward silences, but I am grateful for the silences, because I am that much closer to getting what keeps me alive. And though we don't connect in the ways I have, and do, with my therapists, I am okay with our lack of connection, because in the end, I get what I need.

Sweet, Soft Life, I Love You

have a problem with softness,
In that I am not.

Acknowledgments:

Thank you to the following publications, in which versions of these essays first appeared:

Split Lip Magazine: "The Blow Dryer Is Full of Souls and Other Facts in Lists," originally published as "The Hair Dryer is Full of Souls & Other Facts in Lists"

The Rumpus: "God Circle"

Hobart: "Dear   , I'm Sorry I Exist," originally published as "Apologies"

It's hard to know where to begin when it comes to thanking those that had a hand in the creation of *The Ways She Feels*, as writing this book was nowhere close to a solitary act. But because I have to start somewhere, I want to give a big shout out to what laid the foundation to make writing this book possible: Lexapro for keeping me alive, Vyvanse for making it possible for me to focus (even if only for a few hours each day), and the "lofi hip hop music - beats to relax/study to" Spotify playlist made by user ChilledCow, which my mom likes to call "spa music," for creating the ideal writing soundtrack, albeit spa-like.

My mom, Trish Cook, is also a writer and once dedicated a book to me (and my sister, but that's beside the point). Though I haven't quite returned the favor, I'd like to thank her endlessly here for her support both in my writing pursuits and in my life in general. Mom–I'm sorry I absolutely traumatized the shit out of you for the first ~15 years of my life, but I hope the years of struggles were worth it to get where we are now. You are my best friend and twin flame and other half and the reason why I am who I am, which is why I once had a friend meet you and then tell me "so that's why you are the way you are!" to which I said, "hell yeah!!!" I will keep saying that "hell yeah" forever.

Thank you to my sister Kelsey for being the funniest person alive and for fiercely defending me any time someone dared to be mean to me, because if they'd known me at all they should've known they were entering a world of trouble with Kel by my side. In her words, I may be "too much of a pussy" to stand up for myself, but Kel has enough fire for the both of us. Kel, I know you don't read books, but maybe try and read this one? Just a thought. If you made it this far, send me a text saying "pickle." Yes, this is a test.

Thank you to my dad, Steve, who has always told me that "hard work equals big rewards," and made sure I didn't only hear that, but internalized it. Without him I never would have believed in myself enough to write any of these essays, no less this book. Thank you, Dad, for making me push myself, never letting me quit, and always telling me that I'm a rock star. Even though it's been difficult to grapple with the fact that you've never viewed yourself as sick even when you were so obviously ill on many occasions, I appreciate you showing me that just because I struggle with a certain illness doesn't mean I have to be the "sick girl." You taught me that I am always Courtney before anything else.

Thank you to my grandma, Mimi, for always wanting to read my work and never shying away from my (at times) horrifically honest and raunchy way of writing. I don't know of anyone else I'd rather eat ramen, drink beer, and yell at Republicans on TV with. I am so glad I called you to come pick me up after Mom and Dad didn't answer that time at the beach when I was fourteen and thought I was going to poop my pants any second. Thank you for letting me use your bathroom, and then hanging out with me for hours and telling me things you'd never even told Mom. Mom, sorry because I know you're still jealous.

I am eternally grateful for all the amazing teachers I've had who have helped me find and hone my voice as a writer and as a human. Special thanks goes to University of Michigan professors Jaimien Delp and Susan Rosegrant for encouraging me when I was first beginning to write nonfiction and had no clue what I was doing. Jaimien, your guidance and comments in first drafts was instrumental. Susan, I appreciate you not saying anything that time I had a panic attack during workshop and had to do pigeon pose on the floor of your classroom until it passed.

Of course, thank you thank you thank you to the University of California, Riverside's MFA program. I appreciate every member of my cohort who read my work and all the professors who helped me take this book from point A to point 12, as they can testify that what I sought out to write, and the book you're now holding, are two very different works that don't even exist in the same universe. I simply couldn't have done it without the support of Reza Aslan, Emily Rapp Black, Katie Ford, and Tom Lutz. I cannot express how much it meant to me that when I started submitting weird, illustrated works to workshop, y'all just went with it and never told me I wasn't "literary enough," or that I or my work didn't belong. Thank you for letting me be me and never (openly) getting annoyed when I brought my 13.5-year-old cocker spaniel to workshop, even when she snored. A lot.

Most importantly, thank you to all of Tin House. You have been a dream and a half to work with, and I'd do it again in heartbeat (speaking of: do ya wanna?). To everyone who had a hand in making this book of mine as beautiful as it is–Win McCormack, Craig Popelars, Masie Cochran, Diane Chonette, Elizabeth DeMeo, Alyssa Ogi, Becky Kraemer, Nanci McCloskey, Yashwina Canter, Anne Horowitz, David Caligiuri–you're superstars. Seriously.

Thank you to all my friends who let me send them drafts of my essays with comments that ranged from "I think I may have written a masterpiece???" to "this is the worst thing anyone has ever written it's true garbage can you read anyway haha" and were always willing to read said work and tell me whether I was right, wrong, or somewhere in-between. I want to name y'all but I worry that if I do, it'll be similar to when you knit your partner a sweater, or get a tattoo of their name, and then it places a curse on your relationship and you immediately break up. Instead, I will say: you know who you are and I love you enough to not want to jeopardize our friendship by putting your name in writing. Thank you for accepting my weird.

Obviously, thank you to every mental health professional who has treated me and every treatment center I've ever had the privilege of attending. I may have hated you in the moment but there is no doubt in my mind you saved my life. Sometimes it's hard to know what's best for ourselves. You knew when I didn't. Thanks for making me listen.

And in no particular order or for any real reason other than words of affirmation being my favorite love language, thank you to Muttville Senior Dog Rescue, Eggo brand waffles, Skeeps, all my exes and the people I thought were my partners but weren't so they can't count as actual exes, leftists on Twitter, Fruity Pebbles, those really cute and fuzzy Ugg slippers, my BFF mary jane, whoever created the concept of naps, pink hair dye, Kitty Devore Rescue, emo music, orgasms, all the psychics I've seen at Laguna Beach's Chakra Shack (except for the one who told me I would be widowed by 40 because I am still mad at her), and Tom from Myspace.